Why Learn Maths?

The Bedford Way Papers Series

Why Learn Maths?

Edited by
Steve Bramall and John White

Bedford Way Papers

INSTITUTE OF
EDUCATION
UNIVERSITY OF LONDON

First published in 2000 by the Institute of Education, University of London,
20 Bedford Way, London WC1H 0AL
www.ioe.ac.uk

Pursuing Excellence in Education

British Library Cataloguing in Publication Data:
A catalogue record for this publication is available from the British Library

ISBN 0 85473 617 4

Design and Typography by Joan Rose
Cover design by Tim McPhee
Page make-up by Cambridge Photosetting Services, Cambridge

Production services by
Book Production Consultants plc, Cambridge

Printed by Watkiss Studios Ltd, Biggleswade, Beds

Contents

List of Contributors

Richard Aldrich, Professor of History of Education, Institute of Education, University of London

Eric Blaire, Local Education Authority Inspector of Mathematics, London Borough of Hillingdon

Tendayi Bloom, A level mathematics student

Steve Bramall, Lecturer in Philosophy of Education, Institute of Education, University of London

David Crook, Lecturer in History of Education, Institute of Education, University of London

Paul Ernest, Professor of Mathematical Education, University of Exeter

Peter Huckstep, Senior Lecturer in Mathematics Education and Co-ordinator of Primary Mathematics, Homerton College, University of Cambridge

John MacBeath OBE, Director, Centre for Research and Consultancy, Faculty of Education, Strathclyde University

Tony Parsons, Head of Mathematics, Streatham Hill and Clapham High School, London

Richard Smith, Reader in Education, University of Durham

John White, Professor of Philosophy of Education, Institute of Education, University of London

A. Susan Williams, Lecturer in History of Education, Institute of Education, University of London

List of abbreviations

DfEE	Department for Education and Employment
HMI	Her Majesty's Inspectorate
ICT	information and communication technology
LEA	Local Education Authority
MAG	Mathematics Applicable Group
PGCE	Post-Graduate Certificate in Education
QCA	Qualifications and Curriculum Authority
SMP	School Mathematics Project
TIMMS	Third International Science and Mathematics Study

Introduction and overview

Steve Bramall and John White

'What is half of three-quarters?' repeated a clearly embarrassed Mr Woodhead. [He had been asked this question on a radio programme.] 'I would have to think quite hard about that. I am going to delay. I am certainly not going to fall into the mistake that ministers fell into and make a mistake on that ... .' (*The Guardian*, 15 October 1999)

The Senior Chief Inspector is not the only one who has had problems reactivating his school arithmetic: the then Department for Education and Employment (DfEE) minister Stephen Byers failed on 7×8, and David Blunkett took a painful 14 seconds on air to work out 12×9.

Any temptation towards *Schadenfreude* might well be tempered by sympathy from those of us who would also struggle to multiply without the aid of a calculator. But these gaffes illustrate serious policy issues. Mathematics is seen as one of the most important school subjects; but how much of what is learned is actively used by adults? How important is it for living a successful and fulfilling life? Has its educational power been overrated?

Across the globe, mathematics has a privileged place in the school curriculum. This is certainly true of the National Curriculum in England and Wales. Together with English and science, it is one of its three 'core' subjects and is compulsory for all pupils from the age of five to 16. Along with literacy, numeracy is currently the focus of the British government's drive to raise educational standards. The target is that by the year 2002 three-quarters of pupils leaving primary school will be competent in basic mathematics.

We tend to take it for granted that mathematics deserves its prestigious position in education. If pressed to give reasons, we would not be at a loss. Where would people be in the modern world if they could not add up, multiply and calculate percentages? What would become of the national economy in the global market-place if the high-tech industries on which it increasingly relies could not count on a supply of mathematically competent recruits to staff it at different levels?

But what happens if we try to push the argument further? Do these utilitarian reasons for learning mathematics stand up to critical scrutiny? Do they exhaust the ways in which learning mathematics can be justified? What about non-utilitarian justifications – to do with finding pleasure in mathematical thinking for its own sake, or with the place of mathematics in the culture? Are all the arguments which have been put forward in its defence equally sound?

A second group of questions is about the extent of the mathematics that should be taught in schools. Do the arguments that support the teaching of mathematics justify its status as a compulsory subject? Do they provide a sound basis for teaching the subject throughout a pupil's schooling? Should all pupils have to continue to study it once they have mastered the basics? What priority should it have in the curriculum compared with other subjects?

The ten chapters in this book explore these questions and the historical background against which they have been raised. Together, they investigate the varied aims of learning and teaching mathematics and examine the extent to which the discipline deserves the high curricular status it has traditionally enjoyed.

Chapter One, by Paul Ernest (Professor of Mathematical Education at the University of Exeter), examines alternative ways of justifying the teaching of mathematics by relating them to the context of social and political values. The chapter begins by describing several different kinds of mathematics that can be learned and arguing that justifications of mathematics teaching must accommodate this diversity. Ernest questions the utility of academic and school mathematics as a means of achieving desirable educational aims in the modern world. In so doing, he provides arguments against the utilitarian justification as a basis for compulsion. Whilst he judges the technological empowerment provided by mathematics teaching to be overvalued, Ernest feels that the appreciation of mathematics is undervalued. In positive mode he makes a case for raising awareness of the cultural and aesthetic significance of mathematics as a justifiable educational aim. At the same time, he has doubts about whether the subject should remain compulsory for older secondary students for whom learning it has been an unhappy experience hitherto.

Richard Smith is Reader in Education at the University of Durham. In Chapter Two, he challenges the utilitarian justification for learning any more than basic mathematics and argues that the compulsion to study mathematics beyond that point is educationally counterproductive. Smith is a strong advocate of the educational value of mathematics, presenting arguments in its favour stimulated by his classroom reflections on a selection of impressive and profoundly educational experiences. In the first part of the chapter, he shares with us some mathematical puzzles which exemplify this experience. He uses them to demonstrate his contention that mathematics should be valued because it generates insights that are significant and personal. For example it helps individuals to see for themselves that something is the case as opposed to being told about it. Mathematics is presented as a distinctive form of thought, as powerful and beautiful and as an important human achievement. Post-compulsory mathematics is argued to be the better vehicle by which both the motivation to learn mathematics and the appreciation of the value of mathematics can be promoted.

Richard Aldrich is Professor of History of Education and Dr David Crook Lecturer in History of Education at the Institute of Education. In Chapter Three, they present an historical perspective on the place of mathematical knowledge in the curriculum. Their researches begin with a contrast between the practical interest of the Egyptians in arithmetic and the Greek interest in mathematics more widely as revelatory of cosmic reality. This dualism has continued through the history of the subject in Britain since 1500. University mathematics apart, applied mathematics, especially arithmetic, was seen until the nineteenth century as a low-status subject, 'unsuitable for a gentleman and inappropriate for a lady'. Aldrich and Crook trace the increasingly important place of mathematics and arithmetic in school curricula over the last 150 years, culminating in the present government's numeracy strategy.

Steve Bramall teaches Philosophy of Education at the Institute of Education, University of London. In Chapter Four, he casts doubt, from a philosophical perspective, on the special status accorded to mathematics in the curriculum. He argues that utilitarian justifications for learning mathematics are not strong enough to support the curriculum policy of singling out mathematics as more important than other school subjects. Drawing on a philosophical description of the differences between mathematical and other sorts of knowledge and on arguments in favour of the logical priority of ends over means in purposeful human activity, he contends that other subjects are at least equally as important as mathematics for human flourishing. He concludes that a curriculum that privileges mathematics leads to an education that does not satisfy the knowledge requirements for living well in our sort of society. On this basis, he argues for a more balanced relationship between mathematics and other subjects in the curriculum.

Chapter Five breaks the monopoly on masculine voices heard throughout this collection. It not only introduces two women writers, but also throws new light on our lead question 'Why learn mathematics?' by looking at this from the perspective of gender. Tendayi Bloom is an A level mathematics student who is applying to universities to study a maths-related subject. A. Susan Williams is Lecturer in History of Education at the Institute of Education. She is also Tendayi Bloom's mother. Their chapter begins by tracing the recent gender-reversal in mathematical achievement, with girls now outstripping boys at GCSE in a subject seen throughout history as a male domain. Most of the essay takes the form of a dialogue between the authors. This discusses the pervasiveness of mathematics in domestic life – in which women have traditionally had a larger role than men; as well as the continuing dominance of boys in post-GCSE mathematics where vocational considerations come more into play.

John White is Professor of Philosophy of Education at the Institute of Education. In Chapter Six, he asks 'Should mathematics be compulsory for all until the age of 16?' The chapter examines reasons given for studying the subject to see if they are powerful enough to generate a positive answer to this question. White looks first at non-instrumental reasons, separating the less well-founded of these, for example those to do with the training of the mind (see Chapter Seven), from more adequate ones, for example those to do with the intrinsic delights of the subject and its place in human culture. Instrumental reasons have to do with the everyday uses of arithmetic, vocational requirements and the mathematical equipment people need as citizens. The conclusion from this review is that there is no strong case for compulsory mathematics beyond the first two or three years of secondary school. Voluntary courses could be introduced for those keen to go further. (See also Chapters Two and Ten.)

Chapter Seven incorporates the three perspectives from which the other contributions to this book have been written – philosophy, history and contemporary mathematical education. The author of the chapter, Peter Huckstep, is Senior Lecturer in Mathematics Education at Homerton College, University of Cambridge, where he helps to prepare teachers of primary mathematics. He has also completed a doctorate in philosophy of education at the Institute of Education in London on the aims of mathematics education. Chapter Seven provides a critical assessment of the claim that learning mathematics helps to train the mind. He contrasts Plato's defence of this, connected with wider insight into the nature of reality, with the view, originating with Descartes and found in the work of Fitch and Tate through to recent Her Majesty's Inspectorate (HMI) reports, that mathematics helps one to think logically in other departments of life. He concludes that the most defensible version of the 'mental training' argument, Thomas Tate's, supports mathematics teaching at the place where it is least in need of legitimizing argument – at the elementary level.

Eric Blaire is a Local Education Authority Inspector of Mathematics for the London Borough of Hillingdon and also a philosopher of education with a doctorate on the nature of mathematics and mathematics education.

In Chapter Eight, he defends the compulsory status of mathematics, arguing against the sceptical positions of Steve Bramall, Richard Smith and John White. As an alternative, he puts forward an interpretation of the nature and value of mathematics that, he argues, justifies compulsion for all throughout schooling. In this positive contribution, he presents mathematics as the science of possibilities, a disciplined and imaginative process of conjecture about possible worlds. Understood this way, mathematical thinking is argued to be essential to thinking about the natural and social world and, therefore, an indispensable element in everyone's education and in every phase of schooling.

Chapter Nine presents the viewpoint of a practising mathematics teacher. Tony Parsons is Head of Mathematics at Streatham Hill and Clapham High School. The chapter is entitled 'Another mathematician's apology' after G.H. Hardy's classic text, and is a celebration of the value of mathematics – especially its intrinsic delights – by someone deeply committed to his subject and to its teaching. Tony Parsons distances himself from the sceptical views of the three philosophers on whose contributions he was asked to comment. He also rejects the mechanical way in which the subject has often been taught and is well aware of the negative feelings, including fear of failure, which many students consequently feel towards it. However, these obstacles 'are not reasons for dropping mathematics from the compulsory curriculum, but for rediscovering the meanings of mathematics and education'.

The last word is with another sceptic, although not this time a philosopher. Professor John MacBeath is a researcher on school organization and school effectiveness, who directs the Centre for Research and Consultancy in the Faculty of Education at Strathclyde University. Originally a modern linguist, since 1997 he has been a member of the government's Task Force on Standards chaired by David Blunkett. Chapter Ten begins from his own foiled attempts as a schoolboy to find an answer to the question 'Why do we have to do mathematics, sir?' In his view the educational system has traditionally encouraged both pupils and teachers to accept 'the way it spozed to be' without questioning it. John MacBeath reviews the claims of other school subjects to a place in the curricular sun and wonders why, given the strength of these, mathematics (along with English) is seen as sacrosanct. In the absence of good reasons for its compulsory status as a discrete subject at secondary level, 'heretical though it might be, we might consider secondary school mathematics as a potentially attractive extra-curricular activity'.

This book began life within the history and philosophy academic group at the Institute of Education, University of London. It originated within its Broader Perspectives Unit, set up in late 1997 to explore current issues in educational policy on which the two disciplines could be usefully brought to bear. The historians and philosophers of education who participated in the project then joined forces with a teacher of mathematics, an A level student of the subject, a local education authority (LEA) mathematics inspector, a professor of mathematics education, and a leading figure in the world of school effectiveness research to write this book.

The structure of the book reflects a balance between mathematical insiders and outsiders. Just over half of the contributors are non-mathematicians.

Books and articles about the nature and purposes of mathematics education have traditionally been written by mathematics specialists. However, what place mathematics should have in schools is not a question for which those within mathematics education can provide authoritative answers. It is an issue for all citizens. This is because it is inextricable from wider matters to do with what the aims of school education in general should be. This latter question is political. It can only be answered with reference to wider questions about the sort of society we want and how individual members of society may lead flourishing lives.

Mathematics insiders do have a special role to play in the articulation of issues concerning mathematics education. Pronouncements from outside need to be made on the basis of adequate information about the nature of mathematics and mathematics education. At the very least, they need to be tested against the judgment of professionals in order to see whether they are sufficiently in touch with the world of school mathematics. Yet insiders have a further role. They are familiar as *professionals* with the question of 'Why learn mathematics?' Reflection on the rationale for this belongs to their specialized intellectual equipment. This does not give them a privileged voice on an issue which is, as we have said, ultimately political. However, it does mean that those who participate in the political debate would do well to pay full attention to the views of people whose professional commitments have led them to think more deeply and more often about the aims of mathematics education than laypersons.

The range of views in this collection about the place of mathematics in the curriculum reflects the diversity of backgrounds of the contributors. At one end of the spectrum is John MacBeath's view that secondary school mathematics might become an extra-curricular activity; and at the other are Eric Blaire's belief that mathematics should be compulsory for as long as school is compulsory even 'if that age were ten or 20', and Tony Parson's conclusion that 'there is less justification for non-compulsory mathematics than for non-compulsory English'.

The often stark clash of opinions in this book is good news for the reader looking for a stimulus to think more deeply about the question of 'Why learn mathematics?' This is true whether he or she is a mathematics educator or someone outside the discipline – a parent, teacher, student or policy-maker. The stimulus is needed precisely because the place of mathematics is so commonly taken for granted.

None of the contributors is a blind supporter of the status quo in mathematics education. None denies that, as things are, the subject is, for many older pupils especially, boring or pointless and that the more obvious utilitarian justifications for it are not enough to grant it its favoured position in the curriculum. Several of the mathematicians among the authors seem to suggest that the answer lies in teaching the subject more adequately, so that pupils are motivated to grasp currently neglected values, especially intrinsic values and links with other parts of the culture. One of these mathematicians, Paul Ernest, and several of the non-mathematicians ask whether, in the perceived absence of good enough reasons for making it compulsory until the age of 16, mathematics might be voluntary for older students.

In the new curricular age into which Britain is entering at the threshold of the twenty-first century – with a new National Curriculum equipped, not before time, with a humane and comprehensive statement of overall aims, the credentials of every traditional curriculum subject will henceforth have to be checked against these. Is it an adequate vehicle to enable these aims to be realized? Will parts of it have to be jettisoned? Can it be justified as a compulsory subject rather than a voluntary activity and for what age groups?

The wider re-evaluation of the school curriculum which the new millennium looks set to usher in is likely to penetrate even the 'core' of the curriculum, as currently understood. Even mathematics.

1 Why teach mathematics?

Paul Ernest
University of Exeter, United Kingdom

Why teach mathematics? What are the purposes, goals, justifications and reasons for teaching mathematics? How can current mathematical teaching plans and practices be justified? What might be the rationale for reformed, future or possible approaches for mathematics teaching? What should be the reason for teaching mathematics, if it is to be taught at all? These questions begin to indicate the scope of what Niss (1996) has termed the 'justification problem' for mathematics teaching.

Before discussing the aims of teaching mathematics, there are three theses that I wish to assert as having an important bearing on this discussion. These concern, first of all, the lack of uniqueness and multiplicity of school mathematics; second, the current overestimation of the utility of academic mathematics; third, the socially and societally embedded nature of the aims of teaching and learning of mathematics. Acknowledging these claims means that the discursive space to be occupied differs from that in many traditional discussions of the aims of mathematics education.

The multiplicity of school mathematics

First of all, I want to argue that school mathematics is neither uniquely defined nor value-free and culture-free. School mathematics is not the same as academic or research mathematics, but a recontextualized selection from the parent discipline, which itself is a multiplicity (Davis and Hersh, 1980). Some of the content of school mathematics has no place in the discipline proper but is drawn from the history and popular practices of mathematics, such as the study of percentages (Ernest, 1986). Which parts are selected and what values and purposes underpin that selection and the way it is structured must materially determine the nature of school mathematics. Further changes are brought about by choices about how school mathematics should be sequenced, taught and assessed. Thus, the nature of school mathematics is to a greater or lesser extent open, and consequently the justification problem must accommodate this diversity. So the justification problem should address the rationale not only for the teaching and learning of mathematics, but also for the selection of what mathematics should be taught and how, as these questions are inseparable from the problem.

The utility of academic mathematics is overestimated

Second, I wish to argue that the utility of academic and school mathematics in the modern world is greatly overestimated, and the utilitarian argument provides a poor justification for the universal teaching of the subject throughout the years of compulsory schooling. Thus, although it is widely assumed that academic mathematics drives the social applications of mathematics in such areas as education, government, commerce and industry, this is an inversion of history. Five thousand years ago in Ancient Mesopotamia, it was the rulers' need for scribes to tax and regulate commerce that led to the setting up of scribal schools in which mathematical methods and problems were systematized. This led to the founding of the academic discipline of mathematics.

> the creation of mathematics in Sumer was specifically a product of that school institution which was able to create knowledge, to create the tools whereby to formulate and transmit knowledge, and to systematize knowledge.   (Høyrup, 1987: 45)

Since this origin, pure mathematics has emerged and has sometimes been internally driven, either within this tradition (such as scribal problem-posing and problem-solving in Mesopotamia and Ancient Egypt) or outside of it (such as the Ancient Greeks' separation of pure geometry explored by philosophers from practical 'logistic'). Nevertheless, practical mathematics has maintained a continuous and a vitally important life outside of the academy, in the worlds of government, administration and commerce. Even today, the highly mathematical studies of accountancy, actuarial studies, management science and information technology applications are mostly undertaken within professional or commercial institutions outside of the academy and with little immediate input from academic mathematics.

However, the received view is that academic mathematics drives its more commercial, practical or popular 'applications'. This ignores the fact that a two-way formative dialectical relationship exists between mathematics as practised within and without the academy. For example, overweight and underweight bales of goods are understood to have given rise to the plus and minus signs in medieval Italy. However, it was the acceptance of negative roots to equations in Renaissance Italy that finally forced the recognition of the negative integers as numbers.

The mathematization of modern society and modern life has been growing exponentially, so that by now virtually the whole range of human activities and institutions are conceptualized and regulated numerically, including sport, popular media, health, education, government, politics, business, commercial production and science. Many aspects of modern society are regulated by deeply embedded complex numerical and algebraic systems, such as supermarket checkout tills with automated bill production, stock control; tax systems; welfare benefit systems; industrial, agricultural and educational subsidy systems; voting systems; and stock-market systems. These automated systems carry out complex tasks of information capture, policy implementation and resource allocation. Niss (1983) named this the 'formatting power' of mathematics and Skovsmose (1994) terms the systems involved, which are embedded in social practices, the 'realized abstractions'. The point is that complex mathematics is used to regulate many aspects of our lives – our finances, banking and bank accounts – with very little human scrutiny and intervention once the systems are in place.

Furthermore, individuals' conceptualizations of their lives and the world about them is through a highly quantified framework. The requirement for efficient workers and employees to regulate material production profitably necessitated the structuring and control of space and time (Taylor, 1911) and for workers' self-identities to be constructed and constituted through this structured space-time-economics frame (Foucault, 1976). We understand our lives through the conceptual meshes of the clock, calendar, working timetables, travel planning and timetables, finances and currencies, insurance, pensions, tax, measurements of weight, length, area and volume, graphical and geometric representations, etc. This positions individuals as regulated subjects and workers in an information-controlling society/state, as consumers in post-modern consumerist society, and as beings in a quantified universe.

In the era of late- or post-modernism a new mathematics-related ontology or 'root metaphor' (Pepper, 1948), has become dominant in the perceptions of the public and powerful in society. In particular, my claim is that the accountant's balance-sheet and the world of finance has come to be seen as representing the ultimate reality. Although elements of such a social critique are well anticipated in Critical Theory (e.g. Marcuse, 1964; Young, 1979), this perspective has not so often been turned around and used to critique mathematics itself.

My claim is that the overt role of academic mathematics – that which we recognize as mathematics *per se* – in this state of affairs is over-played. It is management science, information technology applications, accountancy, actuarial studies and economics that are the source for and inform this massive mathematization on the social scale.

This has important consequences for the justification problem, as it means that although there is undoubtedly an information revolution taking place, increased mathematical knowledge is not needed by most of the population to cope with their new roles as regulated subjects, workers and consumers. More mathematics skills beyond the basic are not needed among the general populace in industrialized societies to 'cope' with these changes, if to 'cope' means, as here, to serve rather than to critically master, which is discussed below. Thus, national success in international studies of mathematical achievement is not the creator of economic success, unless having compliant subjects and consumers is what is needed. Of course, there is a need for a small elite who control the information systems and mechanisms, and a group of specialist technicians to service or programme them. These need to be present in all industrialized societies. However, this group represents a tiny minority within society and their very special needs should not determine the goals of mathematics education for all. In addition, if this analysis is correct, it is not academic mathematics which is so very useful and needed for the information revolution. It is instead a collection of technical mathematized subjects and practices which are largely institutionalized and taught – or acquired in practice – outside of the academy.

In summary, my claim is that higher mathematical knowledge and competence, i.e. beyond the level of numeracy achieved at primary or elementary school, is not needed by the majority of the populace to ensure the economic success of modern industrialized society. Although other justifications for school mathematics can be given, and indeed will be given below, the traditional utilitarian argument is no longer valid. Most of the public do not need advanced mathematical understanding for economic reasons, and the minority who do apply mathematics acquire much of their useful knowledge in institutions outside of academia or schooling. This has been termed the 'relevance paradox', because of the 'simultaneous objective relevance and subjective irrelevance of mathematics' in society (Niss, 1994: 371). Society is increasingly mathematized, but this operates at a level invisible to most of its members.

The aims of teaching mathematics are socially and societally embedded

Third, I want to claim that the aims of mathematics teaching cannot be meaningfully considered in isolation from their social context. Aims are expressions of intent, and intentions belong to groups or individuals. Educational aims are thus the expression of the values, interests, and even the ideologies of certain individuals or groups. Furthermore, the interests and ideologies of some such groups are in conflict. Elsewhere, building on Raymond Williams's (1961) seminal analysis, I distinguish five interest groups in the history of educational and social thought in Britain and show that each has distinct aims for mathematics education and different views of the nature of mathematics (Ernest, 1991). These groups and their aims are summarized in Table 1, below.

Table 1 *Five interest groups and their aims for mathematics teaching*

Interest group	Social location	Mathematical aims
1 Industrial trainers	Radical 'New Right' conservative politicians and petty bourgeois	Acquiring basic mathematical skills and numeracy and social training in obedience (authoritarian, basic-skills-centred)
2 Technological pragmatists	Meritocratic industry-centred industrialists, managers, etc, New Labour	Learning basic skills and learning to solve practical problems with mathematics and information technology (industry- and work-centred)
3 Old humanist	Conservative mathematicians preserving rigour of proof and purity of mathematics	Understanding and capability in advanced mathematics, with some appreciation of mathematics (pure-mathematics-centred)
4 Progressive educators	Professionals, liberal educators, Welfare State supporters	Gaining confidence, creativity and self-expression through mathematics (child-centred progressivist)
5 Public educators	Democratic socialists and radical reformers concerned with social justice and inequality	Empowerment of learners as critical and mathematically literate citizens in society (empowerment and social justice concerns)

These different social groups have been engaged in a contest over the National Curriculum in mathematics, since the late 1980s (Brown, 1996).

In brief, the first three more reactionary groups managed to win a place for their aims in the curriculum. The fourth group (progressive educators) reconciled themselves with the inclusion of a personal-knowledge-application dimension, namely the processes of 'Using and Applying Mathematics', constituting one of the National Curriculum attainment targets. However instead of representing progressive self-realization aims through mathematics this component embodies utilitarian aims: the practical skills of being able to apply mathematics to solve work-related problems with mathematics. Despite this concession over the nature of the process element included in the curriculum, the scope of the element has been reduced over successive revisions and is currently being totally eliminated.

The public educators' aim, concerning the development of critical citizenship and empowerment for social change and equality through mathematics, has played no part in the National Curriculum (and is absent from most other curriculum developments too). Thus, although progressives see mathematics within the context of the individual's experience, the notion that the individual is socially located in an unjust world in which citizens must play an active role in critiquing and righting wrongs plays no part.

The outcome of the historical contests and processes is that the National Curriculum may be said to serve three main purposes. First of all, much of the National Curriculum in mathematics is devoted to communicating numeracy and basic mathematical skills and knowledge across the range of mathematical topics comprising number, algebra, shape and space (geometry and measures), and handling data (incorporating information technology mathematics, probability and statistics).

Second, for advanced or high-attaining students, the understanding and use of these areas of mathematics at higher levels is included as a goal. Thus, there is an initiation into a set of academic symbolic practices of mathematics *for the few* (e.g. General Certificate of Education advanced level studies for 16–18 year olds).

Third, there is (or rather was, as it is soon to be radically reduced) a practical, process strand running through the National Curriculum mathematics which is intended to develop the utilitarian skills of using and applying mathematics to 'real world' problems.

Each of these three outcomes is to a greater or lesser extent utilitarian, because they develop general or specialist mathematics skills and capabilities, which are either decontextualized – equipping the learner with useful tools – or are applied to practical problems. The slant of this outcome comes as a surprise to no-one, because the whole thrust of the National Curriculum is recognized as being directed towards scientific and technological competence and capability. New Labour's education policy has maintained this thrust.

Capability versus appreciation

In technology education, curriculum theorists distinguish between developing technological capability, on the one hand, and appreciation or awareness, on the other (Jeffery, 1988). In brief, technology capability consists of the knowledge and skills that are involved in planning and making artefacts and systems. Technology appreciation and awareness comprises the higher-level skills, knowledge and judgment necessary to evaluate the significance, import and value of technological artefacts and systems within their social, scientific, technological, environmental, economic and moral contexts.

An analogous distinction can be applied to mathematics which suggests the following question. Is school mathematics all about capability, i.e. 'doing', or could there be an appreciation element that was overlooked in the National Curriculum? There is a well-known view that 'mathematics is not a spectator sport', that is, it is about solving problems, performing algorithms and procedures, computing solutions, and so on. Except in the popular domain, or in the fields of social science or humanities which comment on mathematics as opposed to doing mathematics, nobody reads mathematics books, they work through them. Furthermore, the language of both school and research mathematics are full of imperatives, ordering the reader to do something, rather than follow a narrative (Rotman, 1993; Ernest, 1998). Thus, the capability dimension of mathematics, and of school mathematics in particular, is dominant and perhaps universal.

Of course, if mathematics is to be given a major role in the curriculum, as it almost invariably is, some large capability element is necessary, as unquestionably knowledge of mathematics as a language and an instrument does require being able to work and apply it. Furthermore, a minimal mathematical capability is essential, a *sine qua non*, for the development of mathematical appreciation. But is capability enough on its own? Has any published curriculum addressed anything else, such as appreciation? Would the development of mathematical appreciation be a worthwhile and justifiable goal for school mathematics? If so, what is mathematical appreciation and how could appreciation be addressed?

The first issue that needs to be addressed is what the 'appreciation of mathematics' means. In my view, a provisional analysis of what the appreciation of mathematics understood broadly, might mean, involves the following elements of awareness:

1 having a qualitative understanding some of the big ideas of mathematics, such as infinity, symmetry, structure, recursion, proof, chaos and randomness;
2 being able to understand the main branches and concepts of mathematics and having a sense of their interconnections, interdependencies and the overall unity of mathematics;
3 understanding that there are multiple views of the nature of mathematics and that there is controversy over its philosophical foundations;
4 being aware of how and the extent to which mathematical thinking permeates everyday and shopfloor life and current affairs, even if it is not called mathematics;
5 critically understanding the uses of mathematics in society: to identify, interpret, evaluate and critique the mathematics embedded in social and political systems and claims, from advertisements to government and interest-group pronouncements;
6 being aware of the historical development of mathematics, the social contexts of the origins of mathematical concepts, symbolism, theories and problems; and

7 having a sense of mathematics as a central element of culture, art and
   life, present and past, which permeates and underpins science, technology and all aspects of human culture.

In short, the appreciation of mathematics involves understanding and
having an awareness of its nature and value, as well as understanding and
being able to critique its social uses. The breadth of knowledge and
understanding involved is potentially immense, but many learners leave
school without ever having been exposed to, or thought about, several of
these seven areas of appreciation.
   My purpose in contrasting capability and appreciation in mathematics
is to draw attention to the neglect of the latter, both in theory and practice. To be a mathematically literate citizen, able to critique the social
uses of mathematics, which is the aim of the public educator position
summarized above, would go part way towards realizing mathematical
appreciation, if it were implemented. However, there would still be a
further element lacking, even if this were to be achieved. This is the
development of an appreciation of mathematics as an element of culture,
and of the inner culture and nature of mathematics itself. Despite the love
for mathematics felt by most mathematics teachers, educators and mathematicians, the fostering of mathematical appreciation, in this sense, as
an aim of mathematical teaching, is not promoted. Therefore, it might be
said that mathematics professionals both undervalue their subject and
underestimate the ability of their students to appreciate it.

Conclusion

To summarize, four main aims for school mathematics have been discussed above.

1 To reproduce mathematical skill and knowledge-based capability
The typical traditional reproductive mathematics curriculum has focused
exclusively on this first aim, comprising a narrow reading of mathematical capability. At the highest level, not always realized, the learner learns

to answer questions posed by the teacher or text. As is argued elsewhere (Ernest, 1991) this serves not only to reproduce mathematical knowledge and skills in the learner, but to reproduce the social order and social injustice as well.

2 To develop creative capabilities in mathematics

The progressive mathematics teaching movement has added a second aim, to allow the learner to be creative and express him or herself in mathematics, via problem-solving, investigational work, using a variety of representations, and so on. This allows the learner to pose mathematical questions, puzzles and problems, as well as to solve them. This notion adds the idea of creative personal development and the skills of mathematical questioning as a goal of schooling, but remains trapped in an individualistic ideology that fails to acknowledge the social and societal contexts of schooling, and thus tacitly endorses the social status quo.

3 To develop empowering mathematical capabilities and a critical appreciation of the social applications and uses of mathematics

Critical mathematics education adds in a third aim – the empowerment of the learner through the development of critical mathematical literacy capabilities and the critical appreciation of the mathematics embedded in social and political contexts. Thus the empowered learner will not only be able to pose and solve mathematical questions, but also be able to address important questions relating to the broad range of social uses (and abuses) of mathematics. This is a radical perspective and set of aims concerned both with the political and social empowerment of the learner and with the promotion of social justice, and which is realized almost nowhere in mainstream school education. However, the focus in the appreciation element developed in this perspective is on the external social contexts of mathematics. Admittedly, these may include the history of mathematics and its past and present cultural contexts, but these do not represent any full treatment of mathematical appreciation.

4 To develop an inner appreciation of mathematics – its big ideas and nature

This fourth aim adds a further dimension of mathematical appreciation, namely the inner appreciation of mathematics, including the big ideas and nature of mathematics. The appreciation of mathematics as making a unique contribution to human culture with special concepts and a powerful aesthetic of its own, is an aim for school mathematics often neglected by mathematicians and users of mathematics alike. It is common for persons like these to emphasize capability at the expense of appreciation, and external applications at the expense of its inner nature and values. One mistake that may be made in this connection is the assumption that an inner appreciation of mathematics cannot be developed without capability. Thus, according to this assumption, the student cannot appreciate infinity, proof, catastrophe theory and chaos, for example, unless they have developed capability in these high-level mathematical topics, which is out of the question at school. The fourth aim questions this assumption and suggests that an inner appreciation of mathematics is not only possible but desirable to some degree for all students at school.

The justification problem in mathematics education is problematic, partly because any so-called solution can only be a partial set of arguments concerning the role of mathematics teaching and learning for a certain clientele (the learners), in certain countries, during a certain timeframe, satisfying the supporters of one or more viewpoints. Thus, part of the problem is its shifting and relative nature. Another part of the problem is that mathematics is simultaneously undervalued and overvalued in modern western society. It is overvalued because, first of all, its perceived utility is misunderstood to mean that all persons need maximal knowledge and skills in mathematics to function economically. However, the mathematics underpinning the functioning of modern society is largely embedded and invisible. Second, mathematical attainment is mistakenly identified with intelligence and mental power and used to grade and select persons for various forms of work, including professional occupations, as well as in terms of suitability for higher education.

Because of this role, mathematics serves as a 'critical filter' and has been implicated in denying equal opportunities to many (Sells, 1973).

Mathematics also is undervalued because most justifications in support of its continued central role in education are based on extrinsic arguments framed in terms of utility and instrumentality. As an intrinsically valuable area of human culture, mathematics is rich in intellectually challenging and exciting concepts including infinity, chaos and chance. It is an imaginary realm and domain of knowledge with its own aesthetics and beauty. Mathematics also has a central part to play in philosophy, art, science, technology, information technology and the social sciences. Appreciation of this is surely part of every learner's entitlement, while he or she is studying mathematics.

The mention of student entitlements raises an as yet unaddressed question. Should mathematics be taught throughout the years of compulsory schooling and should the same curriculum be followed by all? Requiring learners to study mathematics from the age of five to 16 years is less easy to justify if mathematics is not as useful as is often assumed. Furthermore, if it is an unhappy learning experience for almost half of the population as research suggests, should not learners themselves be given some say in the matter, perhaps after having acquired basic mathematical competency? Should not the changing personal preferences, career interests and vocational development plans that emerge in students during adolescence be accommodated, by a differentiated mathematics curriculum or by allowing students to opt out altogether? If education is to contribute to the development of autonomous and mature citizens, able to participate fully in modern society, then it should allow elements of choice and self-determination. However, in the space available here I can only raise these crucial issues, rather than treating them thoroughly.

Finally, let me add a remark on the gap between the domain of discourse on aims and the practical domain in which the impact of educational practices is experienced. However noble, high-flown, or otherwise intentioned the aims of mathematics teaching may be, they need to be evaluated in the light of their impact on individuals and society. Any consideration of the mathematics curriculum requires that three levels must be considered (Robitaille and Garden, 1989). These are the levels of, first, the intentional or planned curriculum; second, that of the implemented or enacted curriculum; and, third, that of the learned curriculum including learner outcomes and gains (including affective responses). The extent to which goals of mathematics education are implemented and realized in classroom practice is a major determinant of the nature of the mathematics teaching in classrooms. Teaching is an intentional activity and, ideally, there should be a strong relation between the expressed aims and the realized practices of mathematics education. Where this link fails to obtain, there is an area of disequilibrium and inconsistency which creates stresses for teachers and students. Of course, this can be reactionary in a site where traditional conceptions and practices subvert well-justified curriculum plans. However it can also be a site of resistance where aims locally deemed unworthy or unpopular are subverted. This, once again, raises the issue of which group's values and views are dominant in determining the aims of teaching mathematics, and who gains and who loses.

2 Insight and assurance

Richard Smith

> When someone is trying to teach us mathematics, he will not begin
> by assuring us that he *knows* that $a + b = b + a$.
>
> (Wittgenstein, 1977: § 113)

I

Such credentials as I have for writing about mathematics and mathematics
education are, whatever else they may be, not mathematical ones. Formal
mathematics ceased for me after O level, and my encounters with the
mathematics curriculum since then have been mainly through my children
and their homework. Their mathematics strikes me as more interesting
than mine was. However it is still far from clear to me exactly why they
are studying it. What is it *for*? Why, above all, is it compulsory throughout the whole of compulsory schooling?

Instead of confronting these questions straightaway, I want to describe
four pieces of non-compulsory mathematics: three occasions when mathematics, not pursued as part of any formal syllabus, has been experienced
as *impressive*. Three of the examples come from a mixed-discipline
group of students on a one-year Post-Graduate Certificate in Education
(PGCE) Secondary course, and one is from my own primary schooling.
In every case, the students and I looked back on these experiences as
among the most profoundly *educational* moments of our lives. When we
talked about these experiences we tried to tease out what it was about

them that made them educational, and the answers that we tentatively reached are sketched here. In the second section of this chapter, I will suggest that if such experiences as these really are valuable, then if they are to be more widespread there are implications for the curricular status of mathematics.

In the first example, a friend demonstrated to the student in her second year at university the proof of the irrationality of $\sqrt{2}$. It cannot be expressed as the ratio of two natural numbers (n/m) without absurdity. The proof goes as follows. We start by assuming that $\sqrt{2}$ is rational (i.e. the opposite of what we want to prove), and assuming further that n/m is in its lowest terms (i.e. it has been cancelled down).

1 n and m cannot both be even, or $n/m = n'/m'$ (e.g. if $n/m = 2/6$ then n/m = 1/3).
2 If $\sqrt{2}$ is a rational number, then $\sqrt{2} = n/m$.
3 If $\sqrt{2} = n/m$, then, by squaring, $2 = n^2/m^2$.
4 If $2 = n^2/m^2$, then $2m^2 = n^2$.
5 If $2m^2 = n^2$, then n is even.
6 If n is even, then there must be a natural number such that $n = 2a$.
7 Therefore, $2m^2 = n^2 = 4a^2$.
8 Therefore, $m^2 = 2a^2$.
9 Therefore, m is even, which (together with (5) above), contradicts (1).

Now this, it seemed to the student then and to her and most of her peers as they went over it together more recently, is ingenious. It is neat, economical and elegant. The satisfaction of following it is akin to that of following a well worked-out detective plot – a Sherlock Holmes story, perhaps, in which the solution is both overwhelmingly *necessary* and at the same time esoteric, even exotic ('When you have demonstrated that every other solution is impossible, Watson, the remaining one, however implausible, must be correct'). Thus, too, in a chess problem, mate in three may begin by moving a pawn one square, on the opposite side of the board from where the action appears to be taking place. One's notion of proof, of the nature of logic as opposed to what merely seems obviously to be the case ('surely the thing to do is to get the King in check with the

Queen'), of the satisfaction of proving something with a measure of panache, is nourished by such things.

The second example is as follows. A philosophy lecturer, guesting on a social science course, was trying to get a first-year class to see just what new ways of thinking the Enlightenment brought; in particular, the idea that you didn't need to rely on authorities, you didn't need to have things interpreted for you – you could see them for yourself. *Sapere aude.*

> A monk sets out to climb a mountain one day. He sets off at dawn. After a while he stops to eat his breakfast. A little later, he has a rest, then he stops for some time to admire a rare plant, answer the call of nature, read the *Church Times*, what you will. He reaches the top of the mountain at dusk, communes with whatever power he has climbed to commune with, and sleeps under a pile of leaves. Next morning, he begins his descent at dawn. No packed breakfast, no newspaper to read; much easier going down than up. He reaches his monastery, from which he had set off, in time for lunch. Now, is there any time at which he is at the same height on both days? And if he is, is this a matter of chance, or a matter of necessity? If he isn't, is it because it is *impossible* that he should be at the same height at the same time?

The reader who cannot quickly see the answer (and who is, be reassured, in good company) ought certainly, for the sake of the satisfaction waiting at the end, to ponder the question for several days at least. As they say on the television news, if you don't want to know the result, then look away now. The solution becomes clear – doesn't it? – if you construct a graph of the monk's ascent and descent (time along one axis and height along another). The lines must cross. Compare the situation where I drive from Bristol to Swindon and you drive in the opposite direction on the same day. Unless one of us starts after the other has arrived, it must be that we pass on the motorway. We must be, at some instant, at the same point at the same time. You see this, when you see it, for yourself. Descartes, that quintessential Enlightenment thinker, dabbled with graphs to some effect – we still talk of 'Cartesian co-ordinates'. Here, notwithstanding the reservations of post-modernists and other critics of the Enlightenment legacy, there seems to be a stride forward in the progress of humankind.

Authorities are seen to be unnecessary, and intellectual power and human dignity stand on a new footing.

The third example is from propositional logic. If p then q ('If the team is relegated then the manager will lose his job') can be symbolized as $p \supset q$. The meaning of $\supset$, the 'material implication' sign ('If p then q' is the same as saying that 'p materially implies q'), is given by the following 'truth-table':

p	q	$p \supset q$	
T	T	T T	T
T	F	T F	F
F	T	F T	T
F	F	F F	T

That is to say, the material implication holds where both p and q are true, not where p is true but q is false (not where the team is relegated but the manager doesn't lose his job) and so on. The truth-table must be the same as that for $\sim(p.\sim q)$, where $\sim$ is the negative sign and . the sign for conjunction. $\sim(p.\sim q)$, which in the example above can be read as 'You can't have the situation where the team is relegated and the manager isn't sacked', is equivalent to $p \supset q$; the truth-table for $\sim(p.\sim q)$, to omit here lengthy demonstration, is clearly that given in the table above. So that table *must* be the table for $p \supset q$. However, the third line of the truth-table brings the odd and counter-intuitive consequence that we seem to have to say that the false proposition implies the true one: that the implication holds where the team is not relegated but the manager is sacked nevertheless. Clearly, on one level, this seems sensible – the manager might be sacked for other reasons. Yet one is left with the niggling feeling that there is something unsatisfactory about the idea that material implication holds where the antecedent (p) is false and the consequent (q) is true. How, to repeat, can a false proposition imply a true one?

Here the impressive thing is to see logic (as a branch of mathematics) struggling to find an adequate way to formalize an aspect of language. One sees mathematics in the process of being born, so to speak; sees it as something *invented* by human beings for human purposes, not as something unfathomably given (like French irregular verbs, perhaps) which for some reason or another we have to accommodate ourselves to. Perhaps this is the place to note that it is not 'discovery learning', in the usual senses of that phrase, that is at issue here. One no more discovers that $a + b = b + a$ than knows it by being told it.

Finally, my own example is as follows. In the last year of primary school, Mr Stevens drew a horizontal line on the blackboard. 'This,' he told us, 'is ten inches long.' Marking it roughly half-way along its length he labelled the left-hand portion a and the right-hand portion b. 'Now [in a voice heavy with significance – this was clearly no ordinary question] how long is b?' The confident consensus was that the answer was five inches (we could certainly have been described as concrete operators). 'But mightn't b be four and three-quarters of an inch, or five and one-eighths?' Bewilderment descended, until one Andrew G. had the crucial insight (so impressed was I that I remember every detail). The answer was $10 - a$: this was all you could say about b. Some of the class found they could share this insight immediately; there was some exasperated shaking of heads. The line stayed on the board for some weeks. Occasionally, Mr Stevens would smile at it and then at us (good teaching occurs sometimes in fairly odd ways). Although this took place during conventional schooling, there was something about the occasion that told us this was different, that we wouldn't need this for the 11 plus. Mr Stevens was given to such irrelevancies, usually on a Friday afternoon. 'What would happen if an unstoppable object met an immovable one?' I was 20 years old before I could comfortably dissolve *that* question.

I would describe the excitement here as something like discovering another language, another kind of truth. In the language of a certain version of developmental psychology it was, of course, the stirring of 'formal operations'. Mathematics, it appeared, was not just about finding determinate answers and not just about measuring or calculating. There was, I think, something of the sense of risk about the whole business of algebra, as it developed: a sense rather like that of tightrope-walking, with none of the reassurance that there would be a clear and definite answer – £3.7s.6d., say – at the end. When later I came across the idea in literary criticism of the rejection of *closure*, the insistence that a reading of a poem does not aim to reach a definitive interpretation but rather consists in the tension between a number of different readings, the idea seemed oddly reminiscent of algebra. Nowadays when I teach ethics I find the first task is to get students to see that moral philosophy does not aim principally at establishing a once-and-for-all answer to questions such as 'Is abortion right or wrong?' Rather it is a matter of understanding, for example, that if your views on abortion rest on a notion of the sanctity of all human life then you need a convincing account of what distinguishes human life from the pre-human form, and a 'pro-life' stance on abortion may sit rather oddly with particular attitudes to war or euthanasia. The value and function of certain variables, so to speak, holds implications for that of others; and sometimes it may not be possible to go beyond formal statements of relations between moral positions, the ethical equivalent of $b = 10 - a$. (I do not say that this is the only possible view of ethics, nor that my own view is exhausted by this account.)

I would prefer these examples to speak for themselves rather than to speak further for them (it would be ironic to try to *assure* the reader). However, a little more advocacy may make my central point clearer. The mathematical insight that lies at the heart of each example – and the more than just mathematical insight, as I have tried to indicate – turns on seeing for oneself. As Wittgenstein says in the remark at the head of this chapter, it is no good anyone assuring us that it is the case. That would short-circuit the whole business and destroy it, just as surely as when someone tells us 'what the poem means'. Seeing for oneself here takes time. On the teacher's part, it requires patience and a kind of faith that the learner will voluntarily return to the topic (prompted, of course, by whatever means the teacher devises to help this along), will be sufficiently engrossed to dwell on and explore it. This is not the world of the more old-fashioned mathematics classroom, with its premium on getting the answers right and moving on to the next set of problems and the techniques for solving them.

II

Some primary headteachers take a brisk approach to literacy. 'We make sure they learn to read,' one said to me grimly, 'just like you'd make sure your own kids learned to cross the road safely. It's the same point: you can't survive in the modern world without it.' She went on to expound further her own philosophy of literacy. She made a sharp distinction between basic, functional literacy and the kind that sees a child reading novels for pleasure or coming to enjoy a performance of Shakespeare. In between the two kinds, she held, there was the approach to literacy which is neither the one thing nor the other, but which most of the developed world is obsessed by.

> I call it forced-marching them along the literacy road, from the green readers to the blue to the yellow or whatever. When what difference does it make if the child has a reading age of 13.7 or 13.6? She's already literate enough to read the bus timetable or fill in the forms, and the forced-march may improve your school's scores on some national scale, but it's probably a good way to make sure the child never becomes a lifelong lover of books and reading.

Variations on this philosophy might be appropriate to other subjects of the curriculum, and I want to sketch here the case for applying it to mathematics. It bears strongly on the justification for the place of mathematics on the curriculum, and on how we justify the subject to children. The mathematics PGCE students I meet invariably offer as the justification for their subject that it is 'useful', 'you need it in the real world' and so on. (This seems to be very common – see, for instance, Andrews, 1998.) What follows is predictable: the modern linguists, historians and so on insist that they have never had the slightest use for most of the mathematics that got them their GCSEs or O levels. Simultaneous equations for some reason get a severe mauling. Meanwhile, the mathematicians maintain with increasing desperation that we would be lost without differential calculus, Fibonacci numbers, matrices or trigonometry, in the face of relentless assertions from their colleagues that they have safely and successfully reached the age of 22 or 37 years without having had the slightest use for such things. ('But suppose you were constructing a bridge in a developing country' went one last-ditch attempt to defend – I think – trigonometry, to groans of disbelief.)

I am not suggesting that the utilitarian justification for mathematics is not a good one. On the contrary, it is obvious that there are very power-ful utilitarian grounds for certain parts of mathematics; it would be perverse to suppose otherwise. We are talking here, of course, about the mathematics that is *commonly* useful. There are no doubt parts of math-ematics which are useful for undergraduate physicists or actuaries to know, but the justification for teaching these parts of mathematics to everyone on these grounds is no better than that for teaching everyone Latin on the grounds that some will become archaeologists or archivists. However, the sharper the exclusively *utilitarian* criteria for including mathematical knowledge and techniques in the curriculum the smaller that curriculum appears to be. What is incontrovertibly useful and pre-vents us from being swindled in shops or from missing trains or putting too much flour into our cake recipes is of relatively small scope. Basic arithmetic and mensuration make a case for themselves with little diffi-culty, but beyond that the case for inclusion is by no means clear-cut. Certainly, much of the GCSE curriculum looks as if it would have a hard time justifying itself on utilitarian grounds. There is no doubt consider-able room for those with more mathematical and pedagogical knowledge than I have to debate what should and should not be included.

Once we make this (possibly over-) sharp division, separating off the 'commonly useful' part of mathematics, we achieve a number of things. First, as with basic literacy, we remove the gulf separating compulsory school mathematics from the ordinary adult world. The mathematics children learn in this part of the curriculum is the same mathematics that they see their parents and others using outside the school as they add up items on a bill or work out how many rolls of wallpaper to buy or mentally convert dollars into pounds on the family holiday. The justifi-cation of the subject then becomes straightforward and honest. We also here achieve a kind of clarity of focus. As with the primary headteacher's approach to literacy above, we should be able to work with greater confidence and determination in our efforts to instil (it might well and very properly be a matter of instilling, to use that unfashionable term) 'essential mathematics'. The idea of the 'basics', so often a cause of confusion and muddied waters, actually seems quite helpful here.

Another and more important result of reducing the compulsory part of mathematics to the incontrovertibly useful, and the result I want to concentrate on here, concerns what it might be possible to achieve in the rest of the mathematics syllabus, the part which would be taken as an option (on a par with, say, German). The four examples which I gave in the first section of this chapter came, in every case, from outside of any formal mathematics syllabus and from non-mathematicians teaching non-mathematicians. They came from a friend scribbling on a piece of paper in a pub, from a social science foundation course, from pursuing a side-track in philosophical logic beyond the edge of the syllabus, from a primary teacher leaving his pupils something intriguing to think about over the weekend. One conclusion that could be drawn here is, of course, that anything potentially interesting is killed by being incorporated into a formal syllabus, but I think that that is the wrong conclusion. Certainly, the conclusion that each of the students and the rest of the seminar group came to was that school mathematics had been just a matter of 'learning to turn the handle to grind out the results'. Even the mathematicians in the group, soon to become professional teachers of mathematics in secondary schools, recognized this description and were happy to describe themselves in the same way, for example 'I just seem to have a facility for turning the handle and getting the answers' and similar descriptions.

Released from the relentless drive to inculcate techniques, post-compulsory mathematics would be free to develop a new kind of syllabus. It would be one capable of revealing to its students the extraordinary power and beauty of mathematics, its distinctiveness as a form of thought, its place as an astonishing achievement of the human mind. It might then become possible to expect educated people to talk about mathematics as warmly and knowledgeably as they do about novels or music or architecture. And what would this almost unimaginable change achieve? Perhaps that individuals who had to acquire new mathematical skills during their working lives came to the task with enthusiasm and the expectation of understanding; that the average person's eyes no longer glazed over at the sight of a table of statistics; in short, that mathematics was widely seen as interesting instead of being, what it manifestly is to so many, an object of fear. Current educational practice seems to construe that fear as largely the result of simple incompetence, and to seek better and better ways of teaching the techniques of mathematics, the business of 'turning the handle'. Once we go beyond basic, 'commonly useful' mathematics, however, it may be that that construal causes more problems than it solves; there is then not even the utilitarian reason for persisting in it.

The comparison with literacy is helpful here. How many 14-year-olds are inspired by their compulsory reading of Shakespeare or Dickens to read them for their own pleasure, and how many are deterred from ever reading them again? If Shakespeare is a breathtaking writer, if he can make you feel that he *knew everything*, then this is precisely a reason for *not* making it compulsory to read him. Compulsory status, whether with literature or mathematics, has the effect of saying 'You'd never do this unless you had to.'

My suggestion, to conclude, is that there are good reasons for releasing those who have acquired the 'commonly useful' basics of mathematics (whatever we decide those are) from any compulsion to pursue the subject further. Beyond the basics, various options can be envisaged: the conventional mathematics syllabus, for those whose interest and talent take this form; the kind of course designed to show the power and beauty of mathematical ideas; courses in the history of mathematics ... the creativity of mathematicians, and their capacity for drawing on their specialist interests in mathematics, would have enormous scope.

There are at least two foreseeable objections. The first, however expressed, will amount to concern that if substantially fewer children achieve good passes in the sort of GCSE mathematics we are familiar with then some sort of 'dumbing down', a decline in standards, has taken place. To this the reply is that it is very hard to see just what kind of standard the present situation – the rapid forgetting of techniques, learned without any true mathematical understanding and never again found necessary by the great majority of people, shortly after they have been acquired – is meant to represent. The second objection is that such new kinds of syllabus will be not mathematics, not the real thing, but something more like 'mathematics studies'. However, this only shows how difficult we find it to conceive of alternatives to the present far from satisfactory state of things: how reluctant we are to see the extent of the problem, and to consider possible solutions.

Acknowledgements

I am grateful to Maria Goulding for discussion helpful in preparing this chapter (and in particular for correcting my shaky mathematics), and to Chris Long for the example of the monk and the mountain.

3 Mathematics, arithmetic and numeracy: an historical perspective

Richard Aldrich and David Crook

Introduction

Mathematics has a strong place in British schools. GCSE figures for 1999 for home candidates showed a total of 672,950 entries for mathematics. This was the largest single subject entry and comfortably ahead of entries for English, the next highest at 638,018 (*The Times*, 26 August 1999). At GCE Advanced level, the situation was reversed. English topped the list with 90,340 entries. Mathematics with 69,945 entries took third place to general studies with 85,338 (*The Times*, 19 August 1999). International comparisons provide a different perspective. A recent survey of nine European countries reported by Edge and West showed that at secondary school level 'the recommended time allocation for mathematics in this country is less than any of the other eight countries studied' (Edge and West, 1998: 62). The Third International Mathematics and Science Study of 1995 covered 40 countries. Although English children performed well in science, in mathematics they were placed twenty-fourth, and Scottish children twenty-eighth (Robinson, 1998: 59–60). Such figures raise several issues. Is too much or too little time being devoted to mathematics? On what grounds should mathematics be taught in schools? How much mathematics do children need to know? Are children being taught the right type of mathematics? Are other subjects being crowded out of the school curriculum by the disproportionate amount of time devoted to mathematics?

This chapter, in common with others in this book, addresses such questions – but from an historical perspective. Historians cannot provide final answers – indeed, there are no final answers – but they can provide data about such issues as how mathematics was understood in the past, what was taught and for what purposes. In so doing, they can identify changes and continuities, and locate the subject of mathematics within broader curricular and cultural contexts.

The control and construction of the school curriculum has a long history. However, such control and construction has also been contested, most recently with respect to the National Curriculum of 1988. Understandably, mathematics teachers, whose own professional careers and professional identities are bound up with the subject, may seek to maintain, and indeed even to strengthen, the central position which mathematics currently occupies within the school curriculum in England. Teachers of subjects which occupy a smaller place or are totally excluded may think otherwise. Similarly, children and adults will be divided in their views as to the importance and utility of mathematics in their lives.

At least four basic positions may be identified with respect to the contemporary argument.

The first is occupied by those who believe that since the invention of the calculator and the computer the need for mental arithmetic has much diminished, and that substantial time previously spent on learning tables and practice in the first four rules of addition, subtraction, multiplication and division would be better devoted to teaching children to think mathematically in a range of situations. In an important recent professorial lecture, entitled *New Cultures, New Numeracies*, Richard Noss argues that although children certainly need to acquire the routine skills of calculation, such numerical facts are 'only a very small part of what mathematics is about, and what it is for' (Noss, 1997: 23). Noss maintains that the current concept of numeracy, which he considers to be shallow in comparison with the concept of literacy, needs to be expanded to include the whole of mathematics. He concludes that for too long mathematics curricula have essentially been about number, and that 'The limitations of old technologies have hung around the necks of mathematics classrooms for 2,000 years, shaping what it was possible to teach, what it was possible to learn'. He suggests that new technologies can provide new learning cultures and techniques, so that it will be possible to supply 'new kinds of mathematical tools designed to make visible the mathematics which lies beneath our social and working lives' (Noss, 1997: 33).

A second position is that routine skills of calculation remain important for every member of the community in the daily challenges of domestic, social and working life. For example, Edward Effros has stated that while calculators have their uses, 'elementary calculations should never be done on a calculator' (Effros, 1998: 135). Such routine skills are particularly important for those who will use a sophisticated application of mathematics in their professional lives. Thus in the letters pages of *The Times*, David Franklin argued in response to Sir Bryan Thwaites:

> I spent 38 years applying mathematics and computing in science, engineering, medicine and commerce, and I had many occasions to be grateful for my mental-arithmetic abilities, based on the by-rote learning Professor Thwaites so dislikes. I also observed my younger colleagues, brought up on a different regime, floundering in arithmetic, and indeed mathematics generally, because they had never been properly taught the tools needed for their work. Facility in mental arithmetic gives confidence in handling numbers and insights into calculations.
>
> (*The Times*, 14 and 17 July 1998)

The third and fourth positions relate to the amount of time spent on the subject. On the one hand are those who, citing international surveys, argue that more time should be devoted to mathematics. Others believe that the position of mathematics in school is already grossly inflated. According to this point of view, numeracy is not as important as literacy. Supporters argue that arithmetic plus some basic elements from geometry will suffice for the great majority of the population. People can use computers for a range of activities, just as they use cars, without having to know how to program them or without even having to understand how they work. The basic mathematics which inform most individuals' social lives consists in calculating the value of commodities in shops, rates of interest on loans and purchases, and the amount of materials needed for a variety of household tasks – from making curtains to feeding the lawn.

This chapter is divided into six further sections. It begins with the issue of definition, followed by that of purpose. These sections are followed by a chronological treatment divided into three periods: early modern, nineteenth and twentieth centuries. Finally, some conclusions are drawn.

Definition

The first historical perspective is one of definition. According to the definitions supplied in a widely used contemporary dictionary, mathematics is:

> The science of numbers and their operations, interrelations, combinations, generalizations, and abstractions and of space configurations and their structure, measurement, transformations, and generalizations.

Arithmetic is 'a branch of mathematics that deals with the operation of addition, multiplication, subtraction and division' (*Longman Dictionary of the English Language*, 1991).

The second, therefore, is defined as a sub-section of the first. This relationship is of long standing, but it could be argued that mathematics and arithmetic are also separate, in that they have distinct historical origins. In respect of 'Western' culture, it has been maintained that mathematics, as defined above, has a definite beginning in history, whereas the origins of mathematics construed principally in an arithmetical sense are lost in the mists of time. John Dubbey has suggested that:

> If we define the term 'mathematics' to be a methodical deductive system of argument from axioms to conclusions, then we can say without much doubt that mathematics was invented by a Greek, most probably Thales of Miletus, around 600 BC. If, on the other hand, we take it to mean any systematic manipulation of size, shape or number, the history goes back as far as we like, certainly beyond anything recorded.
>
> (Dubbey, 1970: 7)

The Greek perception of mathematics and of its relationship to arithmetic is apparent in Plato's *Republic*, written in the fourth century BC, which included a five-fold division of mathematics into arithmetic, astronomy, geometry, solid geometry and harmony. These divisions were recognized across the centuries, for the subjects of study inherited from the Romano-Greek culture of the Ancient world provided the basis for the scholarly curriculum of the Medieval period. The seven liberal arts comprised the trivium of grammar, logic and rhetoric, to which was added the quadrivium of mathematical subjects – arithmetic, astronomy, geometry and music. A key figure in the incorporation of these mathematical subjects was the Roman statesman and philosopher, Boethius (c. 475–524). Boethius is best remembered for his translations of works by Aristotle and for *De Consolatione Philosophiae*, written during a year's imprisonment at Pavia, prior to his execution on grounds of treason. However, Boethius also demonstrated the role of mathematics within a liberal education, and during the Medieval period his textbooks on the four mathematical subjects were widely used in schools, including those in Britain. The most influential of these was *Arithmetic*, which was still in print in the sixteenth century.

Mathematics and arithmetic as studied and employed in the modern era in Britain and other countries of western Europe, however, drew upon traditions from Iran, Syria and India, as well as those of Greece and Rome. By the thirteenth century, Arabic numerals (1, 2, 3) were in use alongside Roman (I, II, III), and algebra (derived from the Arabic *al-jabr*, 'the reduction') provided a means of representing quantities by letters and their relationships by signs. During the same century, the institution of universities at Oxford and Cambridge assisted in a process of curriculum development whereby one of the trivium subjects, namely grammar, became the particular preserve of certain schools for boys. Grammar schools were devoted to the teaching and learning of Latin grammar – the language of classical learning and of the Christian faith and church. Logic and rhetoric were recognized as subjects of study for the bachelor's degree, while the mathematical subjects of the quadrivium were often assigned to the master's level. Although, during the fourteenth and fifteenth centuries, the arts course continued to provide a basic staple of university studies at Oxford and Cambridge, higher faculties of law, both canon and civil, medicine and theology were also introduced.

The distinction between mathematics and arithmetic, therefore, may be sustained both in terms of historical origins and contemporary definitions. Interestingly, these separate identities of arithmetic and mathematics are continued in two contemporary definitions supplied for the single word 'numerate', the adjective derived from 'numeracy':

> Marked by an understanding of the scientific approach and the ability to think quantitatively ... .
>
> *(Longman Dictionary of the English Language,* 1991)

> Understanding basic mathematics and able to use numbers in calculation ... . *(Longman Dictionary of the English Language,* 1991)

Much of today's discussion about the place of mathematics in schools revolves around the concept and definition of numeracy. As Noss has tellingly demonstrated, numeracy as defined in the Crowther Report of 1959 embraced many of the elements of a modern concept of mathematics; at the time of the Cockroft Report of 1982, and subsequently, it was used 'in the narrow sense of the ability to perform basic arithmetic operations' (Noss, 1997: 2).

Purpose

Contemporary definitions and Ancient and Medieval definitions and practice, therefore, provide one starting point for an examination of mathematics in historical perspective. A second is that of purpose.

One fundamental question that has been posed (and on occasion ignored) across the centuries, is 'What knowledge is of most worth?' and therefore should be taught in schools? For example, in 1861 in a book entitled *Education: Intellectual, Moral and Physical*, the railway engineer, philosopher and writer, Herbert Spencer, argued for the primacy of science. This was in sharp contrast to the Clarendon Commissioners whose report of 1864 on the nine leading boys' public schools in England argued for 'the maintenance of classical literature as the staple of English education' (quoted in Maclure, 1969: 87). Contemporary contexts for discussion of curricular purposes include the rapidly increasing amount of knowledge in the world; the rapidly changing means of acquiring, storing, retrieving and communicating such knowledge; the rapidly changing worlds of work; the introduction in 1988 of a national curriculum into maintained schools in England and the subsequent modifications of that curriculum in the light of apparently declining standards in some aspects of the 'basic' subjects of English and mathematics; government directives about general teaching methods (e.g. of the whole-class variety) and about specific subjects (e.g. the learning of tables in mathematics lessons).

This section provides two basic starting points for the consideration of purpose in the teaching and study of mathematics – the first practical, the second philosophical. Clearly, arithmetic has long been useful in commercial and financial dealings. For example, in cultures which had no arithmetical awareness it would have been impossible to calculate the value, whether in terms of barter or money, of more than one sheep or goat at a time. Each would have to be traded separately. In civilizations that flourished before that of Greece – notably in India, China, Egypt and Babylon – mathematical understanding passed well beyond that of simple arithmetic. In Ancient China, for example, although mathematics never became a highly regarded academic discipline, 'merchants learned it for accounting purposes and fortune-tellers studied it to do business through calculations involving astrology' (Leung, 1999: 240). In such early civilizations mathematics was employed for calculating the calendar and for navigation and was used in engineering, notably in the construction of large buildings. The Egyptians were probably the first to recognize that the year consisted of 365 days, while the pyramids, erected in the third millennium BC, exhibited very high levels of accuracy. As Dubbey has noted:

> Sir Flinders Petrie's measurements of the Great Pyramid indicate a maximum error at the corners of only twelve seconds of arc, an accuracy of 1 in 27,000, of the order normally associated with watchmakers rather than structural engineers ... the Babylonians were ... excellent astronomers. Their observations indicate a degree of accuracy unrivalled until post-Copernican times, and their theoretical work makes use of an elaborate system of numerical interpolation.
>
> (Dubbey, 1970: 9, 11)

For the Greeks, however, the prime purpose of mathematics was neither to observe the stars nor to create substantial buildings, though they did both. The Greek 'invention' of mathematics was based upon educational and philosophical foundations. In the protracted education of philosopher kings to enable them to understand the final purpose of philosophy – the idea of the Good – Plato recommended that the period between the ages of 20 and 30 should be devoted to the five branches of mathematics. For the Greeks, mathematics, like philosophy, represented a search for the mathematical structure thought to underlie reality and truth. This search led to a concentration upon geometry, to the neglect of arithmetic and more practical considerations. The Greek concept of the purpose of mathematics was to have a profound influence upon modern mathematics, and upon philosophy, and to find expression in the work of such twentieth-century philosopher mathematicians as Bertrand Russell and A.N. Whitehead. For example, in 1924 Whitehead moved from the post of professor of applied mathematics at Imperial College, London, to that of professor of philosophy at Harvard. The search continues. In 1998 Dales and Oliveri stated categorically that 'The concept of truth occupies a central position both in mathematics and in its philosophy' (Dales and Oliveri, 1998: 1). As Morris Kline has concluded in respect of the Greek influence upon the purpose and methodology of mathematical study:

> The insistence on deduction as the exclusive method of proof, the preference for the abstract as opposed to the particular, and the selection of a most fruitful and highly acceptable set of axioms determined the character of modern mathematics, while the divination and proof of numerous fundamental theorems sent it well on its way.
>
> (Kline, 1987: 79)

The most significant feature of contemporary society, however, is not a renewed search for the mathematical structure of reality for its own sake, but rather for the sake of other ends, for example, security, entertainment and space exploration. The twentieth century has been characterized by unprecedented levels of damage inflicted by some human beings upon others, and upon the planet Earth, and by the rapidity of technological

development. Advanced mathematics has underpinned such development, both in war and peace – from weapons of mass destruction to com-
pact disc drives and the Voyager II probe.

Contemporary justifications of mathematics at advanced levels frequently combine a number of purposes, including that of economic well-
being. For example, the home pages of the School of Mathematics at
Bangor University seek to assure prospective undergraduate students that
it is an interesting, enjoyable, dynamic and practical subject:

> People like its challenge, its clarity, and the fact that you know when
> you are right. The solution of a problem has an excitement and a satis-
> faction. ... You should also be aware of the wide importance of math-
> ematics, and the way in which it is advancing at a spectacular rate.
> Mathematics is about pattern and structure; it is about logical analysis,
> deduction, calculation within these patterns and structures. When patterns
> are found, often in widely different areas of science and technology, the
> mathematics of these patterns can be used to explain and control natural
> happenings and situations. Mathematics has a pervasive influence in
> our everyday lives, and contributes to the wealth of the country.
> (http://hydraulix.bangor.ac.uk/~mas010/public_html/imahob95.html)

Two eminent Cambridge mathematicians have recently portrayed the
importance of the connection between mathematics and economic and
social well-being in more forceful terms. In an article promoting the
Mathematics Millennium Project, John Barrow and Peter Landshoff have
argued that mathematics underpins the several sciences and is essential to
the development of new technologies and their commercial exploitation.
They warn that 'If we neglect mathematics now the consequences will
be far-reaching for business and industry and therefore employment
and society as a whole in the very near future' (Barrow and Landshoff,
1999: 84).

Early modern, 1500–1800

In his classic study, *The Beginnings of the Teaching of Modern Subjects
in England*, first published in 1909, Foster Watson allocated a separate

chapter to each of the subjects – mathematics, arithmetic, geometry and astronomy. Watson's contemporary purpose was to provide a background for the curricula of the county and municipal secondary schools of his day which were coming into being as a result of provisions of the Education Act of 1902. His chapter on arithmetic indicates the ambivalent position of the subject by the seventeenth century. On the one hand, it was a higher subject of great antiquity, one of the four quadrivial arts. On the other, it was a subject that was increasingly associated with the education of the poor and others of lowly status – artisans, clerks and tradesmen – who needed some knowledge of arithmetic to carry on their occupations (Watson, 1909: 288).

The origins of a distinctly British tradition of mathematics are often traced to Robert Recorde (c. 1510-1558). His works on mathematics, including *The Ground of Artes* (1543) and *Whetstone of Wit* (1557), were published in English and were written as dialogues between master and student. The signs of + and – had been first used in the fifteenth century, but Recorde invented the equality sign (=). Born in Wales, Recorde was a physician with degrees from both Oxford and Cambridge. He argued that arithmetic should be studied on two grounds: the antiquity of use in Britain and its practical value. The first chapter of *The Ground of Artes* is dedicated to proving the importance of arithmetic, both as a basis for work in other branches of mathematics and in various occupations, not only those of trade and commerce, but also for lawyers, soldiers and other professionals. In her study of the teaching of arithmetic in Britain across 400 years, Florence Yeldham argued that writers on arithmetic 'almost without exception have followed Recorde in emphasizing the applied side of it' (Yeldham, 1936: 10). Another influential book of the early modern period was Edward Cocker's *Arithmetik*, which first appeared in 1677. By 1750, it had reached a fifty-third edition, and was still in use in the first quarter of the nineteenth century.

Although ancient grammar schools, including those which were to emerge as great or public schools, continued to concentrate upon the study of the classical languages, by the second half of the seventeenth century some new grammar school foundations were prescribing mathematics and arithmetic as subjects of study. Christ's Hospital was originally founded in 1553, but in 1673 a mathematical side for 40 boys was added. These boys were to be taught grammar, arithmetic and navigation, and the school was supplied with an appropriate range of books, maps, globes and mathematical instruments for the purpose. On leaving school at age 16, the boys would be apprenticed to ships' captains for seven years (Watson, 1909: 312). During the eighteenth century, a number of multilateral schools and academies which included the teaching of mathematics were founded, together with others in which mathematics was the prime purpose of study. For example, Nicholas Hans provides details of the mathematical school kept by Thomas Crosby between 1710 and 1750 in New Street in Southwark. Crosby, himself a former pupil of Christ's Hospital, advertised his school as teaching 'Arithmetic, in all its parts, Merchants' Accounts after the Italian method, Algebra, Geometry, Trigonometry, both plain and spherical, Navigation, Astronomy and other parts of Mathematics' (Hans, 1951: 107). The close connection between the growth in mathematical schools and the maritime and commercial worlds is clear. The diarist, Samuel Pepys, who when almost 30 years of age had found it necessary to engage a private tutor to teach him the multiplication tables, and who became secretary to the Navy in 1672, was one of the major supporters of the mathematical school at Christ's Hospital. Thomas Crosby was the author of a text book for merchants, *The London Practice*, and also of a *Complete Treatise on Navigation*. Thomas Haselden, who established a mathematical school in Wapping about 1720, had served for some 16 years in the Merchant and Royal Navies. His publications included *Mathematical Lessons* and a *Daily Assistant to Seamen*.

Nineteenth century

One key element in explaining the central position occupied by mathematics (and particularly arithmetic) in school curricula in England today is to be found in the introduction of the Revised Code of 1862. In the early modern period, and indeed throughout the nineteenth century, religious bodies provided most schools for children of the poor. In such schools, the prime purpose was to teach children to be good Christians and obedient citizens. Acceptance of their lowly station in this life was to be followed by a privileged position in the next. Much of the teaching was oral – and children learned by heart to say the Lord's Prayer, Ten Commandments and Catechism. However, in Protestant countries, including England, it was also thought proper to teach reading, for the specific purpose of reading the Bible and other devotional literature. In the early modern period, writing and arithmetic were recognized as separate and additional skills. Both were taught more frequently to boys than to girls and often for the purpose of securing apprenticeships.

Central government grants for elementary schooling in England had been given since 1833. In 1858 the Newcastle Commission was appointed to examine the state of that schooling and 'to consider and report what measures, if any, are required for the extension of sound and cheap elementary instruction to all classes of the people'. The fact that mathematics, and even arithmetic, were not then regarded as essential elements of the curriculum was clearly revealed.

> Of the children attending the 1,824 public weekday schools visited, only 69.3 per cent were taught arithmetic, 0.6 per cent mechanics, 0.8 per cent algebra and 0.8 per cent Euclid. The corresponding figures for the 3,495 private schools run by individuals were 33.8 per cent, 1.29 per cent, 1.35 per cent and 1.15 per cent respectively.
>
> (Howson, 1982: 120)

This situation was to be changed radically by the introduction of a Revised Code of regulations in 1862. In future, the major part of central government grants to assisted elementary schools would be based on the principle of payment by results. These results would be assessed during an annual visit from one of Her Majesty's Inspectors in the three subjects of reading, writing and arithmetic. Six standards of curriculum and proficiency were established which were intended to correspond to the six years which children might stay in the elementary school (see Table 2).

Table 2 *Standards for arithmetic*

Standard I	Form on black-board or slate, from dictation, figures up to 20; name at sight figures up to 20; add and subtract figures up to 10, orally, from examples on blackboard
Standard II	A sum in simple addition or subtraction, and the multiplication table
Standard III	A sum in any simple rule as far as short division (inclusive)
Standard IV	A sum in compound rules (money)
Standard V	A sum in compound rules (common weights and measures)
Standard VI	A sum in practice or bills of parcels

A major Code revision occurred in 1872. The original Standard I was abolished, so that the first examination of children would now commonly begin at the age of seven. The existing Standards II to VI were re-numbered I to V and a new Standard VI – 'Proportions and fractions (vulgar and decimal)' – was added. The principle of payment by results was modified from 1882 and finally abandoned in 1897. By that date, however, arithmetic's place as one of the essential 3Rs of 'reading, writing and 'rithmetic' was assured. Indeed, given that in the twentieth century the previously separate skills of reading and writing would be merged under the title of 'English', mathematics (which in elementary schools was often still equated with arithmetic) would become one of the two basic subjects.

The Revised Code confirmed the place of arithmetic in the elementary school curriculum. P.B. Ballard, whose career as a teacher and inspector was spent in his native Wales and in London, quoted one headmaster who stated that two-and-a-half hours of each day were regularly devoted to arithmetic. Further exercises would be undertaken in the three months preceding the annual examination, and in some schools it was customary to set the children three examples at 4.30 p.m. and not allow them to go home until the correct answers were given. The Code also confirmed the nature of that arithmetic, which led to ceaseless practice in calculation. For example, around 1890 in Standard IV, sums were set in the three rules of reduction (of money, weights and measures) and multipli-

cation and division of money. Examples of the test questions were as
follows.

1 Reduce 126,987 tons to ounces.
2 Reduce 849,612 drams to cwt.
3 Reduce one million square feet to square poles.
4 £26.15. $7\frac{3}{4}$d × 278
5 £416,073.12.7d ÷ 381 (Gordon and Lawton, 1978: 93)

Meanwhile, in schools for children of the middling and upper classes,
mathematics continued to struggle to find a place. In girls' schools, English,
French and a range of accomplishments frequently provided a central
core. The Clarendon Commission, which in 1864 reported on the nine
great public schools, recommended a mere three hours per week of arithmetic and mathematics. Four years later, the Taunton Commission which
reported on all schools not covered by Newcastle and Clarendon, laid
more emphasis on mathematics. They identified three grades of boys'
schools: those which kept pupils to 18, 16 and 14 years of age. They
recommended that in the second grade more attention should be paid 'to
those subjects which can be turned to practical use in business' including
'arithmetic and the rudiments of mathematics beyond arithmetic'. Parents
of pupils in third-grade schools were seen as wanting 'a clerk's education, namely, a thorough knowledge of arithmetic, and ability to write a
good letter' (quoted in Maclure, 1969: 94–95).

Twentieth century

Regulations for Secondary Schools, issued in 1904, prescribed a curriculum in which a core should be provided in each of three subject areas:
English, including geography and history; languages, ancient and modern;
mathematics and science. A minimum of four-and-a-half hours was to be
given to the first; three-and-a-half for one language and six where two
were taken; and 'not less than seven-and-a-half hours to science and mathematics, of which at least three must be for science' (quoted in Maclure,
1969: 159).

Although the prescriptive nature of these regulations was relaxed in 1907, mathematics had secured that which it had hitherto been denied – a guaranteed place in the secondary school. Between the wars there was considerable discussion over the nature and extent of that place. The Spens Report of 1938 argued for a change in the methods of teaching mathematics so 'that it will no longer be necessary to give the number of hours to the subject that are now generally assumed to be necessary' (quoted in Gordon and Lawton, 1978: 95). Mathematics, however, also had its advocates, and for much of the twentieth century the dominant influence upon the secondary mathematics curriculum was the Mathematical Association. This association was described by Cooper (1985: 90) as 'a body of selective school and university mathematicians founded in the late nineteenth century, originally to promote change in geometry teaching'. School provision for mathematics, however, was uneven. In 1965 statistics published by the Organization for Economic Co-operation and Development (OECD) showed that pupils in the science streams of secondary schools in the United Kingdom spent considerably more time studying mathematics (22 per cent of total time) than pupils in any other OECD country, although those in arts streams spent only 10 per cent (Gordon and Lawton, 1978: 96).

At elementary and primary levels, the centrality of English and mathematics established in the last 40 years of the nineteenth century continued. For example, the 1929 edition of the Board of Education's *Handbook of Suggestions for Teachers* devoted 49 pages to English, together with a further 16 to handwriting, and 48 to 'Arithmetic and Elementary Mathematics', considerably more than for any other subject. More variation in syllabus, however, was encouraged, while practical purposes received considerable emphasis. 'The course of arithmetic for a school where the majority of scholars take up industrial pursuits will differ from that of a school where the majority of scholars pass to commercial life' (Board of Education, 1929: 39). Attention was drawn to gender differences, and while all children should be taught to keep simple accounts, these dimensions of mathematics might assume a particular importance for girls for:

Such tasks as the planning of the weekly, monthly or yearly expenditure of a family, and enquiry into the cost of decorating and furnishing the rooms of a house, or the detailed estimate of outlay during some projected holiday may provide connected work for a series of lessons and will arouse interest because of their reality.

(Board of Education, 1929: 201)

The new mathematics of the 1960s, which followed the launch of Sputnik in 1957 and led to frantic initiatives around the world to improve children's levels of mathematical competence, has been called 'the greatest experiment ever to take place within mathematics education' (Howson, Keitel and Kilpatrick, 1981: vii). New (or modern) mathematics, was characterized by changes in content, structure and pedagogy. Initiatives such as the Individualized Mathematics Instruction Project which began in Sweden in 1964 attracted attention and imitation in many countries. British examples included the School Mathematics Project (SMP) (1961), the Nuffield Mathematics Project (1964) and the Schools Council Mathematics for the Majority Project (1967). From the outset, however, opinions were divided about reform. Cooper (1984: 50–51) records that early SMP proposals attracted criticism both from pure and applied academic mathematicians and draws attention to the title of a particularly critical journal article by Hammersley (1968). During the 1960s and 1970s examples of 'modern mathematics' – sets, statistics, symmetry, translations and Venn diagrams – could be found at every level, from the primary school to the university. Some commentators have linked these changes with the introduction of the Certificate of Secondary Education examination and the drive for secondary comprehensive schools. Others have emphasized that modern mathematics was a 'top down' initiative, led by mathematicians whose concern was for the structures which underpinned so much of the content. The origins of SMP may be traced to a 'coalition of selective and independent school teachers and university mathematicians' whose early aim was to reform traditional GCE Ordinary and Advanced level syllabuses (Cooper, 1985: 89).

Cooper's research (1984: 58) into the introduction of 'modern mathematics' revealed a distinct lack of enthusiasm among former non-graduate secondary modern school teachers, who found SMP irrelevant, 'wordy' and 'time-consuming'. In Cooper's case study comprehensive school it was noted that only the most able groups were exposed to modern mathematics. As for the bottom 30 per cent, the Head of Department commented:

> We must give them success, stuff they can get right. ... They have a limited span of concentration. ... Number work, money, metric units, some appreciation of what you can do with fractions and decimals. ... Any modern topics are strictly for entertainment value only. ... Optimism and confidence-boosting are critical, and accepting that their level of performance will be limited, even in arithmetic.
>
> (Quoted in Cooper, 1984: 59)

In 1982 the Cockroft Report called for the mathematics curriculum to reflect more closely the skills required in further education, employment and adult life. Its critics, however, felt that it was insufficiently rigorous. At the end of the decade, the National Curriculum Working Party for mathematics, chaired by Duncan Graham, later the Chief Executive of the National Curriculum Council, was subject to a schism precipitated by Professor Sig Prais, a personal friend of the then Prime Minister, Margaret Thatcher, an adviser to her Policy Unit, an associate of the Centre for Policy Studies and a formidable champion of traditional content and teaching methods in mathematics (Ball, 1990: 198). Graham's own account (1996: 143–144) describes Prais as a member 'of the school which believed that a thousand long divisions a day are somehow good for the soul, a kind of spiritual experience in their own right'. 'Inevitably,' he adds, 'he [Prais] saw calculators as a manifestation of evil, and wanted them banned to children until the age of 16.' According to Graham, he found himself refereeing a contest between those who sought a return to Victorian methods of arithmetic teaching on the one hand, and the 'lunatic left' which threatened the 'disciplined approach' on the other. Melanie Phillips, however, provided another perspective on this dispute. She criticized Graham both for his approval of the Cockcroft Report and for his treatment of Prais:

> Instead of making use of Prais's unrivalled data and analysis ...
> Graham and his council marginalized him so that before long Prais
> despaired and resigned. In the note of dissent he had previously written
> to the mathematics group's interim report, Prais observed that the
> group's failure to understand that German or Japanese children were
> performing better because they had been properly taught multiplication
> or division or the areas of circles had helped him to understand 'why so
> many of you believe that "having fun" is one of the prime objectives of
> mathematical teaching'.   (Phillips, 1996: 146–147)

In many primary schools, the National Curriculum of 1988 led initially
to a renewed interest in subjects such as geography and history which
frequently had become subsumed into 'topic' work. However, a concern
for 'back to basics' and the restricted nature of the attendant system of
national testing soon emphasized the importance of English and mathematics once more. Similar concerns were expressed about standards and
progression in the core subjects in respect of the secondary school. There
were claims that the relative lack of emphasis in GCSE syllabuses upon
such areas as algebra presented difficulties for students wishing to
proceed to A level and undergraduate mathematical studies. Critics of the
National Curriculum, for example John Marks (1996), continued to argue
that while interactive mathematics might be more fun for pupils, a return
to more traditional approaches and topics held the key to higher standards.

In the early 1990s the potential conflict between raising standards in
English and mathematics on the one hand, and according a substantial
place to all of the designated subjects in the National Curriculum on the
other, became a dominant feature of educational debate. In May 1997 the
balance was tilted by the advent of a Labour government specifically
committed to raising educational standards in literacy and numeracy. The
final report of the Numeracy Task Force, published in July 1998, was
entitled *The Implementation of the National Numeracy Strategy*. Its recom-
mendations ranged from the introduction of a daily 'numeracy hour' in
primary schools to urging the DfEE to make early preparations for the
UNESCO-led World Mathematical Year 2000. In the summer of 1999
considerable progress was recorded towards the government's targets of

80 per cent of 11 year olds reaching Level Four or above in English and 75 per cent in mathematics by 2002. In 1999 Key Stage 2 assessments showed a 70 per cent pass rate in English and 69 per cent in mathematics, as contrasted with 65 per cent and only 59 per cent respectively in 1998 (*The Times*, 16 September 1999).

Conclusions

Four major conclusions may now be drawn.

The first is that 'arithmetic', 'mathematics' and 'numeracy' are not simply interchangeable terms. They have had separate identities and separate historical trajectories. In England since the sixteenth century arithmetic, together with some other of the 'applied' dimensions of mathematics, has been seen as a low status subject – unsuitable for a gentleman and inappropriate for a lady. Until the middle of the nineteenth century even arithmetic had a marginal place in many elementary schools; its centrality was only ensured by the mechanisms and payments of the Revised Code. The relevance of arithmetic (and other elements of mathematics) to the world of commerce, however, was not in doubt. For example, between 1889 and 1937 the pharmaceutical company Beechams Pills Limited distributed more than 45 million copies of the *Beechams Help for Scholars*. This pocket-sized booklet was packed with tables and formulae to encourage proficiency in currency calculations, multiplication, division, factor, geometry and measurement work.

In contrast, the position of 'pure' mathematics, with its Greek ancestry and connections to philosophy, was safeguarded in the ancient universities, and flourished particularly at Cambridge. During the twentieth century, it continued to be seen as an essential and civilizing agent in the science side of secondary schools. Premature specialization, however, meant that mathematics did not acquire a core status throughout all secondary schools. Indeed, in some schools girls were allowed to give up mathematics in favour of another 'science' subject – usually biology.

The reforms of the 1960s and 1970s attempted to bring some of the elite work and accompanying status of mathematics into the schools. For example, the Secondary School Mathematics Curriculum Improvement Study in the USA sought to discard traditional content and sequence in favour of a syllabus that would 'encompass all the mathematics that is now considered essential through a first year university programme, specifically the fundamental structures of number systems and of algebra, linear algebra, probability and its applications, mathematics related to computers and the calculus (analysis)' (Fehr, 1966: 533; quoted in Howson, Keitel and Kilpatrick, 1981: 38). Thirty years later, there has been a reaction against such initiatives. For example, it might be argued that well-meaning efforts to make children calculate using binary numbers in order to reconstruct the logic system of early computers were a distraction from the more essential objective of helping them to solve denary problems. Complaints alleging that children grew up with a knowledge of set theory but unable to add up became legion. The projects of the 1960s have been consigned to the scrap heap and the government's standards for mathematics in primary schools are couched in traditional arithmetical terms, although some would argue at a rather lower level than existed for children of similar ages under the Revised Code.

At the end of the twentieth century, arithmetic and mathematics have been overtaken by numeracy. This term is particularly favoured by a Labour government committed to raising standards of literacy and numeracy. For children in primary schools numeracy has been defined by the Numeracy Task Force as 'a proficiency that involves a confidence and a competence with numbers and measures' (Department for Education and Employment, 1998: 11).

The second conclusion is that the new technologies of the concluding years of the twentieth century have had, and will continue to have, a considerable impact upon teaching and learning and upon all subjects of the school curriculum. This appears to be particularly true of arithmetic. For example, electronic aids have replaced mental or paper and pencil calculations in shops, offices and schools. 'Log tables', invented by the Scot, John Napier in the second decade of the seventeenth century and used by students for more than 300 years, have become obsolete. The new school subject of technology has also impinged upon traditional areas of the curriculum – at times with confusing results. One recent study has indicated that mathematical terminology used in technology lessons may differ from that used in the mathematics classroom. For example, pupils encounter tubes, square corners and dimensions in technology, but cylinders, right angles and measurements in mathematics (Evens and McCormick, 1998).

The third point is that in the year 2000 substantial campaigns have been conducted to promote mathematics as an essential and enjoyable activity. These include the Millennium Mathematics Project, a new national initiative based in Cambridge (Barrow and Landshoff, 1999), and the designation of the year 2000 as World Mathematical Year. Such campaigns must surely emphasize the very significant contributions made over the last 500 years by British mathematicians to international advances, not only in mathematics itself, but also in the fields of science, technology and philosophy. Nevertheless, the call for a new, or renewed, mathematics for the twenty-first century is currently handicapped by two factors. The first is popular (or rather unpopular) memories of and attitudes towards mathematics, whether traditional or new. There is a widespread belief that mathematics is a boring and difficult school subject from which children and adults have been liberated by recent developments in information and communications technology. In consequence, it is argued, the time devoted to it should be significantly reduced. The second concerns the quality of mathematics teachers and teaching. In spite of the core position of mathematics throughout the years of compulsory schooling, numbers and qualifications of mathematics graduates proceeding to posts in teaching, even allowing for the massive increase in the percentage of the population now entering higher education, remain disappointingly low. In 1938 some 75 per cent of all mathematics graduates entered school teaching; in 1988 there were fewer than 10 per cent (Anderson, 1999: 17).

The final conclusion concerns the government's current numeracy strategy. This is focused upon a specific attainment target for 11 year olds and, given the test results of 1999, appears to be working well. Further progress may be anticipated as a result of the introduction of a 'numeracy hour' in primary schools from September 1999. Whether such success will prove to be inspirational or inimical in the development of a more sophisticated concept of mathematics at secondary school and in higher education in the twenty-first century, however, remains to be seen.

Acknowledgements

We are most grateful to John Breakell, Celia Hoyles, Richard Noss, Isobel Randall, John White and Alison Wolf for their comments upon earlier drafts of this chapter.

4 Rethinking the place of mathematical knowledge in the curriculum

Steve Bramall

Introduction

In this chapter I argue that the special status afforded to mathematics in the school curriculum is not warranted by the knowledge requirements of adult life, and that granting mathematics such status can distort a balanced curriculum. The special status of mathematics is questioned both in terms of the claim that an education in mathematics is essential for everyone, and in terms of the belief that mathematics is more important than other curriculum subjects. The argument is made that, whilst the inclusion of mathematics in the curriculum may be justified in terms of its usefulness as a means for helping us to achieve valued goals, other subjects, oriented to ends, merit at least equal weight in curriculum planning.

Mathematics in the curriculum

The current orthodoxy has it that every child ought to study mathematics as a part of his or her schooling. This view echoes that of the 1982 Cockcroft Report which begins with the words:

> There can be no doubt that there is general agreement that every child should study mathematics at school; indeed, the study of mathematics, together with that of English, is regarded by most people as being essential. (Cockcroft, 1982: 1)

The claim that the study of mathematics is an essential part of everyone's schooling is based on the general claim that the use of mathematics is a necessary condition for living a normal or good life in our sort of society, or indeed in many other societies, at the end of the twentieth century. In the Cockcroft Report, as elsewhere, the need for competency in the use of mathematics is described as comparable to the need for competency in the use of English. The argument is that it would be difficult, if not impossible, to live a fulfilling life in a liberal democracy whilst lacking adequate levels of literacy and numeracy.

In addition to the argument that an education in mathematics is essential to everyone's well-being, the Cockcroft Report makes the further claim that the study of mathematics is in some sense more important than the study of other curriculum subjects.

> Mathematics is only one of many subjects which are included in the school curriculum, yet there is greater pressure for children to succeed at mathematics than, for example, at history or geography, even though it is generally accepted that these subjects should form part of the curriculum. This suggests that mathematics is in some way thought to be of especial importance. (Cockcroft, 1982: 1)

The special importance of mathematics implies a special status for mathematics in the school curriculum. The clear inference is that this special status ought to be reflected in perhaps the dedication of relatively high levels of resources, relatively long curriculum time, compulsory status and particular pressure applied to maintaining and increasing standards of achievement in mathematics. Not only is mathematics essential, it is second only to English in the curriculum hierarchy. In a great curriculum balloon debate, one might say that mathematics ought to be one of the last two subjects left in the curriculum basket.

A varied list of reasons is given to justify the special status of mathematics in the curriculum. These reasons include: the necessity of an education in mathematics to further study in the sciences, the need for competency in mathematics to engineering, industry and commerce, and the usefulness of the study of mathematics for the development of powers of logical thinking and spatial awareness. However, none of these applications of an education in mathematics is seen as providing a sufficient justification for granting mathematics its special status within the curriculum. Although not entirely clear in this report, the reasons seem to stem from the observations that: not everyone will go on to the further studies that require a mathematical background, many useful mathematical operations can be done by others or by machine, and there exist numerous alternative means of developing powers of logical thinking and spatial awareness. The only justification deemed adequate for supporting the special status of mathematics comes through the argument that mathematics provides an indispensable and uniquely useful and powerful means of communication:

> We believe that it is the fact that mathematics can be used as a powerful means of communication which provides the principal reason for teaching mathematics to all children.   (Cockcroft, 1982: 1)

Underlying the argument in favour of granting special status to mathematics in the curriculum then is the idea that mathematics is something like a special language with which we can describe, and communicate about, the world.

The claim is then that mathematics provides a means of saying things about the world, or an aspect of the world, that is unique and powerful. Put in more traditional terms, the claim is that mathematics is a particularly fruitful way in which we can gain knowledge about the world. As a means of communication, or as a style of description, mathematics is especially valuable because the information it generates is especially useful to our lives. The author of the report cited above recognizes implicitly the underpinning belief that it is the quality of the knowledge gained through the employment of mathematics that provides the justification for the special status of mathematics:

> Mathematics can be used not only to explain the outcome of an event which has already occurred but also, and perhaps more importantly, to predict the outcome of an event which has yet to take place.
>   (Cockcroft, 1982: 2)

Mathematics then is presented as a favoured means of coming to know things about the world as it is, as it was, and as it will be, which will help us to live better lives. It is this belief in the value of mathematical know-ledge that provides the justification for reserving a special place for the study of mathematics in the curriculum.

The argument that the special value of mathematics derives from the particularity of its purchase on the world reveals a disanalogy between mathematics and English. The natural language of English has very general, if not universal application. That is, we can use English to describe, and communicate about, almost anything. Indeed, it is arguable that English is so universal in its application that it is better described as the medium of communication than a means.[1] Whatever the merits of this claim, it is clear that through a natural language such as English we can talk about the world in almost any of its aspects, and that this is at least partly why competence in one's natural language is so highly valued. Mathematics, on the other hand, delivers a specific sort of knowledge about a specific aspect of the world. In describing and communicating about a specific aspect of the world, mathematics is more like body language, for example, which is primarily concerned with the display and communication of affective states, or the language of colour with which we can describe and communicate about one particular aspect of the world. It is a partial description of the world that reveals phenomena only in their quantitative aspect.

Understanding mathematics as a restricted and limited means of describing and communicating about the world (in contrast to a natural language such as English) implies that a special case (unlike that made for English) has to be made for its special curriculum status. It needs to be demonstrated that understanding the world in its mathematical aspect in particular is of special importance to adults living in a liberal demo-cracy. In Cockcroft's terms, this means showing that the knowledge gained from a mathematical perspective is both essential to everyone, and more important than the knowledge gained from the perspective of any other curriculum subject other than English. In order to investigate the possible grounding for such claims, it will be useful to examine just what sort of description of the world is provided through mathematical representation. We need to know what aspects of what sorts of phenomena are illuminated by mathematics, in short, what are the particular objects of this particular mode of knowing. Once we know this, we may be in a better position to describe the role of mathematics in human well-being and, thereby, better placed to comment on the special status of mathematics in the curriculum.

Mathematical knowledge

Mathematics helps us to gain, manipulate and communicate knowledge pertaining to a particular aspect of reality. Specifically, the symbolic language of mathematics enables us to describe phenomena powerfully and concisely in quantitative terms. Thus, we can represent the spatial and temporal relationships of things, their size, ratio and so on and predict how these might change in the future. Of course, more abstractly, mathematics can talk about itself as a system of representation or about logical possibilities such as infinite size or the square root of negative numbers, but the power of mathematics lies in its usefulness in describing, communicating and predicting the quantitative aspects of things. The usefulness of mathematics comes from its applications in the lived world; in estimating times of arrival, calculating average costs, plotting trajectories, managing finances, using resources efficiently and so on. Mathematics is rich and diverse in tools for thinking about quantity; instruments for measurement, modelling and graphical representation. Clearly, the list of uses and mathematical instruments could go on and on.

When we begin to think of the areas of life for which mathematics is useful, we also begin to see how ubiquitous mathematical application is in human life. It is hard to think of any human experience that is not amenable to mathematical description and analysis. Any phenomena that can be described can be described in terms of quantity. In this sense, mathematics can be said to be universal, a mathematical description can be applied to all things. Even those things which at first sight seem not amenable to mathematical description, for example works of art or feelings, can be described, and often usefully described, as objects with symmetry, regularities, duration and so on.

Mathematical knowledge can also be understood as widespread in the sense that mathematical truths are culturally universal. It doesn't matter whether you're a fifteenth-century English monk or a twentieth-century Native American mother, or a twenty-first-century starship captain, the circumference of a circle will be obtained by multiplying the diameter of the circle by pi. This does not mean that each of these persons necessarily knows this to be the case, indeed they might think otherwise. However, the central truths of mathematics, even if they were generated within one specific culture now have universal application. Immanence does not preclude transcendence.[2] As Siegel writes:

> My arithmetical judgments, for example, though made from my scheme, surely have legitimacy, and are correct, even though small children (for example) do not share either my scheme or my judgments. Important scientific theories similarly have application, and validity, beyond the scheme of those who invented them and their cultural mates – space 'curves', and mass is convertible with energy, for example, even for those whose schemes do not sanction such counter-intuitive judgments. (Siegel, 1995)

In addition to applying to all phenomena, describing and communicating about the world in mathematical symbols is a common human experience, a truly international language.

In addition to its universality, mathematical knowledge has the character of strongly objective knowledge. The truths of mathematics exist as it were 'out there', independent of what any humans may think of them, or in some cases, it could be argued, even whether any humans think of them. Mathematical knowledge can be thought of as lying at the opposite end of the spectrum to subjective knowledge, where by 'subjective' we mean 'personal' or 'from the point of view of a particular individual'. Whether I like blue cheese is a subjective matter. It doesn't make sense to call for a method of verifying whether my personal tastes and preferences are correct. On matters that are purely subjective I am the sole authority. In the case of mathematics the correctness or otherwise of a judgment is wholly divorced from my own subjective persuasion. A correct mathematical judgment is reached not so much by expressing my own views but rather by bringing my beliefs into line with laws and rules and principles that are extant. Our perception of mathematical truths is that they are brute truths, that they constitute part of the hard wiring of the universe. This is the sense in which Plato describes mathematical truths, as eternal and unchanging, as something to be discovered.[3]

Mathematical knowledge is the closest thing to non-negotiable, non-interpretable knowledge that we have. I can't beg to differ with you about the sum of the internal angles of a triangle, or as to whether there's an integer between eight and nine, not that is without risking bringing the idea of rational disagreement into disrepute. We can dispute about which mathematical model will produce the most accurate treasury forecast of movements in the relative value of the pound against other currencies, but in the end one model will turn out to be the better predictor. The dispute in such a case can be settled by empirical demonstration because, although the relative efficacy of mathematical models is contestable, it is not irredeemably or essentially so.

Practical knowledge

Although mathematics (according to the above conception) can supply us with useful, precise, objective and demonstrably correct answers, its use is restricted by the implied relationship between means and ends. In so far as mathematics is concerned only with describing and communicating about the quantitative aspects of phenomena, it can be no more than a means to an end. Mathematics is akin to a tool, and, like any other tool, it is of no help in deciding what job needs, or ought, to be done. No amount of mathematical calculation will produce a decision about the ends of a human life. Such deliberation requires judgments about the desirability of particular aims, goals and purposes. This necessarily brings in statements about values, importance and significance, judgments concerning quality rather than quantity. Furthermore, the most complex mathematical model is unable to represent the meaning of human actions and utterances. Meanings are necessarily contestable and open to interpretation and change. What is good, what is worthwhile, what is important and what things mean then are aspects of reality that can't be grasped from a mathematical perspective. The objects are of a different sort and require other ways of knowing.

The differences in the objects, and in the ways of knowing about the different sorts of object alluded to here can be clarified by looking at the distinction between 'techne' and 'phronesis' made by Aristotle in the *Nicomachean Ethics* (Aristotle, 1976). 'Techne' is the sort of practical rationality suited to deliberating about and determining the best means to a preconceived end (Aristotle, 1976, Book 6). Mathematics, conceived of as a useful tool, can helpfully be understood as 'techne'. 'Techne', for Aristotle is the sort of reasoning that can help us to achieve ends, but it can't be used to decide them. The conception of mathematics presented here also echoes Aristotle's 'techne' in that the rationality of 'techne' can be applied in any situation, it can be brought into any context without having to take into account the peculiarities of that situation. Mathematics also appears to coincide with Aristotle's 'techne' in that it is objective, the individual who is doing the reasoning is detached from the object in question.

In contrast to the technical rationality of 'techne' Aristotle labels the sort of practical rationality suited to moral and political deliberation as 'phronesis'. 'Phronesis' is the sort of rationality that is appropriate to thinking about meaningful and valuable human activities, in particular it is the appropriate reasoning for accompanying the moral and political action that Aristotle believes is the mark of a truly human life. In Aristotle's terms 'phronesis' is concerned with 'what is conducive to the good life generally' (Aristotle, 1976: 209).

It is not simply the case that 'techne' is the rationality suited to deliberating about means and 'phronesis' the rationality suited to deliberating about ends. Rather, 'phronesis' is an action oriented way of knowing or understanding that can cope with the internal relation of means and ends in the determination of moral and political action (Aristotle, 1976). As Gadamer says somewhat cryptically, 'Moral knowledge is really knowledge of a special kind. In a curious way it embraces both means and end, and hence differs from technical knowledge' (Gadamer, 1989: 322). Bernstein fleshes out the argument in *From Hermeneutics to Praxis.*

> Even more important, while technical activity does not require that the means which allow it to arrive at an end be weighed anew on each occasion, that is what is required in moral knowledge. In moral knowledge there can be no prior knowledge of the right means by which we realize the end. For the end itself is only concretely specified in deliberating about the means appropriate to this particular situation.
>
> (Bernstein, 1981/82: 100)

Contextualization of moral knowledge precludes the separation of means and ends, leaving each as a partial co-determinant of the other within the complex of situated moral action.

A second Aristotelian distinction is that, unlike technical reasoning, moral or political reasoning always proceeds in a particular context:

> Again, prudence is not concerned with universals only; it must also take cognizance of particulars, because it is concerned with conduct, and conduct has its sphere in particular circumstances.
>
> (Aristotle, 1976: 212)

What one should do then can only be determined in actual concrete situations. As Gadamer writes:

> What is right, for example, cannot be fully determined independently of the situation that requires a right action from me, whereas the *eidos* of what a craftsman wants to make is fully determined by the use for which it is intended.   (Gadamer, 1989: 317)

Therefore, this kind of practical knowledge is distanced from technical knowledge in that its application cannot be understood merely as the application of a rule or the exercise of a specific skill:

> Moral action must always take into account the exigiencies of each particular concrete situation.   (Gadamer, 1989)

A third relevant feature of 'phronesis' described by Gadamer is put forward in terms of the involvement of the moral or political 'actor'. Gadamer's

point here is that unlike scientific or technical reasoning, 'phronesis'
describes the knowledge or reasoning appertaining to situations one finds
oneself in rather than situations observed:

> For moral knowledge, as Aristotle describes it, is clearly not objective
> knowledge – i.e. the knower is not standing over against a situation that
> he merely observes; he is directly confronted with what he sees. It is
> something that he has to do.   (Gadamer, 1989: 314)

This active involvement of the subject places her or him in the arena
rather than in the audience.

According to this generally Aristotelian approach, when we are confronting the world in the aspect of values, ends, purposeful action and
meanings, the quality of knowledge, and the manner and purpose of coming to know and understand, are unlike those of mathematics. Knowledge
about the meaningful, purposeful and value-laden reality of human moral
and political conduct does not admit of precision. Indeed, in these terms,
it would be a mistake to aim at precision. As Aristotle famously remarked,
'it is the mark of the trained mind never to expect more precision in the
treatment of any subject than the nature of that subject permits' (Aristotle,
1976: 65). Neither should we be aiming at detachment and objectivity.
It is in the nature of moral and political activity that we are involved, and
involved in ways that expressly aim to change the world, as contrasted to
standing back and observing. Interference is in the nature of the game.
A further contrast with the quality of knowledge and way of knowing
associated with mathematics is that 'phronesis' is context-situated rather
than universal. A right decision for one person in one context might be a
wrong decision for someone else in a different context. 'Phronesis' mili-
tates against universal laws or rules of conduct. The truths of 'phronesis'
are always to some degree ambiguous, interpretable and open to future
revision.

From this brief Aristotelian account of the type of knowing that is
characteristic of the world of values, meanings, purposes and actions, it
seems that an education in mathematics will be of severely limited value.
Indeed, it might be argued that, to the extent that mathematics is concerned

with means, and is precise, objective and universal, it is the curriculum subject which is of the very least use to the development of a practical understanding of ends *qua* ends. However, to the extent that the means of achieving ends are, on this formulation, always bound up with the determination of ends, an education in mathematics cannot be lightly dismissed. That said, it seems clear that there exist other curriculum subjects that on the face of it appear more suited to providing the sort of education needed for living an adult life in which deliberation about values, meanings, purposes and actions feature.

One group of candidates is made up of those subjects that help pupils to understand the particularities of the social contexts in which such practical deliberation and action takes place. Immediately one might think of sociology, a subject expressly committed to developing in pupils an awareness and appreciation of the contexts of moral and political action through an understanding of the social structures, processes and institutions within which we act, and which in so doing we help to maintain and transform. Sociology may also be helpful to an education aimed at preparing pupils for the meaningful and value-oriented world of moral and political action in that it is a subject in which pupils can learn the practical methods of generating data about society, and learn to criticize them. Similarly it is a forum in which comparative studies can help to expose the peculiarities of the social structures, institutions and values of one's own, and other societies. In addition, sociology is a subject that can render explicit the methodological complexities of context-situated knowledge and understanding.

Similar cases could be made for other human sciences, which all can be seen as contributing to the sort of education that would prepare children to act in an intelligent and informed manner in the adult world of moral and political action. History can help us to plot the genealogy of our beliefs, values and tools of understanding. It can illustrate through example how ends-oriented moral and political activity comes about and affects the world, and can teach the lessons learned by those who have gone before. History may also help in educating pupils in the methodology of interpretation, and in illustrating the endlessly interpretable nature of the world of meaning. Insofar as moral and political action involves understanding the beliefs, values, feelings and interpretations of others, a case can be made for the need for the inclusion of psychology in an education for moral and political action. The understanding of motives and intentions is important to anyone who aims to care for the well-being of others, and for anyone who wishes to understand their own motivations and their own formation of beliefs and values.

More directly, in a curriculum that aims at preparing children for end-oriented moral and political action, it would seem that there is every reason to include subjects such as morality and politics themselves. The practical understanding of values and their expression through moral and political action, and some experience of moral and political action in a controlled and reflective environment, would seem essential if pupils are to leave school with the ability to develop competence in dealing with the meaningful and valuable ends of human life, as well as with the means of bringing those valued ends to fruition.

Implications for the status of mathematics in the curriculum

The characterization of mathematics as providing exceptionally useful means to the achievement of aims and goals and purposes coupled with the contrasting neo-Aristotelian account of the sort of rationality and practical knowledge that can help us to think and act in the realm of values, ends, morality and politics, may have important implications for the relative place and status of mathematics as a curriculum subject. Whilst it would be misleading to say that mathematics is appropriate to deliberating about means and the social sciences and moral and political studies about ends, it is arguable, given the characterizations presented here, that whereas mathematics can only help to determine the best means, the other subjects mentioned here can at least to some degree help us to think about ends.

In a life that consists of deliberation about both means and ends, orientation to ends is logically prior. It would be absurd to try to work out, mathematically or otherwise, the most efficient or most effective means in the absence of ends to work towards. Indeed, to proceed with the technical rationality of finding efficient and effective means, but without evaluating the ends aimed at, echoes the nightmare scenario of the 'Iron Cage' described by the sociologist Max Weber.[4] Furthermore, whilst it makes logical sense to articulate aims and goals and purposes for which there is no conceivable practical possibility of execution, it makes no sense to talk about the most effective way to bring about a content-free end.

However, the logical priority of the determination of ends over means doesn't necessarily translate into curriculum priority for subjects that are ends-oriented over those (such as mathematics) that are only concerned with means. The first reason for this is philosophical. According to the Aristotelian approach, means and ends in practice are always to some degree co-determinant. Practical ends are restricted by available means, and as we work toward particular ends by employing particular means, new possible ends come into view. The determination of practical ends then always takes place alongside the determination of means. In practice, each is indispensable to the determination of the other. The second reason is that logical priority doesn't imply temporal priority. If I want to write a great novel that will change the world, it may be that the first step is to learn the technical skills of how to use a typewriter. In learning to type, like learning mathematics, I may be preparing to pursue goals later in life that are as yet relatively indeterminate, but which will at a later date become fleshed out. In effect, if and when I do get interested in ends, I will already have the technical means in waiting.

However, in a curriculum that aims to prepare pupils for the broad range of activities and experiences of adult life, it seems that preparation for deliberation about ends ought to be included. There seems to be no good reason why we should prepare pupils with the means to live in the adult world, but not the ability to deliberate about ends. This observation might help in considering the status of mathematics in the curriculum. It seems that there are no good grounds for holding mathematics to be more important or more worthy of curriculum time than subjects oriented towards values, ends, morality and politics. If mathematics is important because it provides some of the means essential to living well as an adult in our sort of society, then sociology or political studies can be said to be equally important in that they are essential to deliberating about the values, ends, morality and politics without which means have no ends.

Furthermore, we can argue that an education in, for example, sociology, which enables individuals to make context-specific moral and political judgments, is necessary for adult life in a stronger sense than mathematics is. Mathematics as a means is potentially substitutable. A calculator, a computer, a friend or an independent financial advisor can substitute for an education in mathematics for instrumental purposes. If mathematics is no more than a means of objectively describing and communicating, then, like any other technical service, mathematical work could be delegated to others. Deliberation about values, ends, morality and politics in contrast cannot. Political and moral responsibility demands that as individuals we each are responsible for our actions, or our delegation of such actions to an executive. I certainly cannot leave it to others to decide what my values are without giving up my much-cherished personal autonomy. Whether mathematics is essential to everyone's adult well-being is disputable, whereas deliberation about values, ends, morality and politics is not, at least that is, if we live in the sort of society where every adult is expected to take responsibility for his or her moral and political actions.

This analysis would suggest that the special curricular status granted to mathematics is unwarranted by the knowledge requirements of adult life in our sort of society. First, whether mathematics is essential to an education to prepare pupils for adulthood is dubious. Second, the claim that mathematics is somehow more important than subjects that aim at developing an understanding of, and competency in, deliberation about meaningful, value-oriented moral and political activity is not sustained. The analysis here would favour a balanced curriculum of subjects that would enable practice in, and reflection on, these latter activities, seen as at least as important as mathematics. One group of subjects that could aid the achievement of a balance between means orientation and ends orientation in the curriculum would be the human sciences, but clearly there would be a number of other candidates not considered here, for example the arts. Giving means-oriented mathematics a special status comparable to that of the universal medium of English and ahead of ends oriented subjects appears perverse. Granting mathematics such a status can only give out misleading signals about the complexities of an adult life that is characterized by the need to act purposively according to one's values in an inescapably moral and political arena. The special status of mathematics in the curriculum seems to rest on a misunderstanding of the different sorts of knowledge and understanding needed for living well in our sort of society. It risks conveying to pupils a distorted picture of the possibilities and responsibilities of an adult human life.

Notes

1   For a discussion about language as a universal medium of understanding, see Gadamer (1989) especially Part III, Section I.
2   For a discussion on the distinction between immanence and transcendence, see Putnam (1981).
3   See Plato (1974).
4   A phrase used by Max Weber (1968) to describe the difficulty of escaping from the means-end, or instrumentalist form of reasoning that he argues is characteristic and dominant in modern rational capitalism.

5 Girls and mathematics

Tendayi Bloom and A. Susan Williams

In the 1990s in Britain, the performance of girls in mathematics started to improve dramatically, both in relation to their previous record and also in relation to boys. This development was unexpected – right up to the last decade of the twentieth century, girls as a group had consistently underachieved in mathematics. Throughout history, indeed, the study of mathematics had been regarded as a male domain, on the grounds that the thinking required for this kind of work was more 'naturally' male than female. 'The idea of mathematics as a male enterprise has always been fundamental to our education,' comments Mary Harris, drawing on the history of the Western world from the sixth century BC to support her argument (Harris, 1997).

The improved performance of girls has generated all sorts of conversations and debates – at the policy-making level, in schools, at work and in the home. One of these conversations was held in the home of the authors of this chapter: between TB, a girl of nearly 18 years of age who is studying mathematics as one of her A level subjects; and ASW, her mother, who is a lecturer in history. They have written down some parts of their conversation in the following pages, as a way of raising questions about this new phenomenon and about the ways in which it has been seen and described. To set the context, some background information will first be given.

Any discussion of *girls* and mathematics is inevitably about *boys* and mathematics, too. The performance of girls in mathematics is nearly always measured in relation to that of boys, and *vice versa* – they are seen to be each other's benchmark. These benchmarks are not equal, however, as boys have always been located in a position of superiority over girls. Yet in the 1970s and 1980s, under the influence of the growing feminist movement, questions started to be asked about the underachievement of girls in mathematics and there was concern that girls were disadvantaged at school in this strand of the curriculum. Research led by Elizabeth Fennema in the USA challenged widely held assumptions about gender differences in mathematics and identified a bias against females among the mathematics education community at large (Fennema, 1990). Dedicated study units were set up to carry out research in the area and numbers of publications were produced. At the Institute of Education, University of London, for example, a Girls and Mathematics Unit was created in the 1980s which led to the writing of *Counting Girls Out: Girls and mathematics* (Walkerdine, 1998).

Then, in the 1990s, the picture started to change and, by 1995, the performance of girls in mathematics was basically similar to that of boys. This improvement was part of a larger overall improvement in which girls were actually outperforming boys at GCSE, in terms of the proportions obtaining five or more higher grade passes. Girls outperformed boys by some considerable distance in English, although in science boys maintained a small advantage (Arnot et al./OFSTED 1998). This development was given massive attention by the media and generated panic among some of the public, who detected 'despair beneath the macho surface' (*Times Educational Supplement*, 15 March 1996) and who feared that boys were being 'lapped by girls' (*Times Educational Supplement*, 14 July 1995). The educational establishment, too, was quick to express concern. In 1994, Chris Woodhead, the Chief Inspector of OFSTED, commented that 'The failure of boys is one of the most disturbing problems we face within the whole educational system' (*Times Educational Supplement*, 15 March 1996).

However, the situation is far more complex than simply a 'failure' of boys. For one thing, the superiority of girls at school is by no means a phenomenon without precedent. When children had to take the 11 plus examination as a way of selecting who would go to grammar, technical and secondary modern schools, girls in many areas achieved higher scores than boys. This achievement was neutralized by the local education authority, which set a quota on the number of girls eligible for entry to grammar school. If the same cut-off mark had been used for both sexes, many more girls than boys would have been educated in grammar schools (Weiner, 1985). Inevitably, children attending grammar schools were guaranteed better opportunities for entry to university and the professions than the children who 'failed' the 11 plus. The main justification for setting a quota on girls was the idea that boys performed less well than girls at the age of 11 because they matured at a slower rate. It was assumed that boys would catch up with girls after puberty and this assumption was supported by the fact that boys outperformed girls at O level, A level and university (Gallagher, 1997).

The recent improvement of girls' performance has shattered assumptions like these. Boys are no longer catching up and in some subjects, they are not even keeping up. The following conversation took place in the light of this kind of change, with particular reference to mathematics.

ASW   It seems unbelievable to me that my own daughter is clever at mathematics and is even applying to university to study engineering.

TB   Yes mum, you would say that [let me interject here to introduce my mother, an ardent feminist, yet sceptical about the entry of females into the area of mathematics]. I do not, however, feel that I have 'clever'-ness, as you said, but more that I have been given opportunities to expand on the inherent feel that people seem to have towards number – opportunities which I have obtained mainly through my formal education.

ASW   But do you think girls and women are comfortable with numbers and mathematics? I know I'm not.

TB   Just recall now how you took me out to a restaurant the other night, and, although wanting to keep the cost of the meal a secret, you felt it necessary to give a proper tip of exactly 15 per cent. Rather than doing the quick sum in your head, you had to show me the bill and let me work it out for you. That just shows how you've had your numeracy submerged and been made to feel uncomfortable about it, even though you can make quick complex calculations about time and distance without thinking about it. For example, you do this when you go marathon running, or when catching a bus or baking a cake.

ASW   I suppose that's true: that I do mathematics all the time without being aware of it. But what does it feel like to you, doing advanced mathematics as a girl? When I was studying for A levels at the start of the 1970s it was still considered peculiar for girls to do mathematics beyond the age of 16 and it never occurred to me to do mathematics, not for one moment. At my school, which as you know was single sex [*TB* So is mine], there were only a few girls taking A level mathematics and the rest of us thought they were terribly brave – pioneers, I suppose. They mostly failed or got low marks, though.

TB   All pioneers, throughout history, have experienced problems – explorers, politicians and scientists, all pushing back the bounds in their own fields, and each experiencing individual pitfalls and disappointments. I greatly admire those students at your school, doing what they did in the face of adversity, and am grateful to them for the legacy which their tentative steps have left for my generation to take up.

ASW   That brings us to the question of 'ought' – ought girls to have to study mathematics up to age of 16, as they do now? What do you think?

TB   *Ought* girls to have to study mathematics up to the age of 16? Ought girls to be educated at all? My view is that girls' education is particularly necessary. I will attempt to explain what I mean, using the stereotypical views so often used in discussions of this kind. The woman is the home-maker, the nurse, the peacekeeper, the chef, and so much more. Nowadays, she is even the breadwinner. It is necessary for her to be well versed in 'womanly disciplines' such as needlework and cooking, for the well-being of the children and husband (let's assume his existence, for now). But then, let's say it promises to be a cold winter, and all three children need new coats. The family have £100 set aside for such a purpose, and it is up to the mother to decide how it should be used. When she takes the children to the shop, they will be clamouring for her attention, each wanting a different pricey item. She could decide to divide the money equally between the three, but that's not fair, because Peter's coats always cost more that the others, because he's reached that age of growth spurt. Perhaps the price of coat varies directly proportionally to size. The mother has entered the shop, and all of this must rush through her head. These dilemmas have always been common for women and they have solved them using their 'women's intuition'.

The studying of mathematics up to the age of 16 can give girls the chance, if not for enjoyment of a stimulating subject, for familiarization and practice in the numerical arts necessary for their lifelong juggling act to come.

ASW   I see what you mean. I suppose there is so much emphasis on the business of studying mathematics at school and the passing of exams, that we forget how important mathematics has always been in domestic life – simply for survival. It's as if school is now considered more important than life!

TB   Good point – let me mention it to my teachers.

ASW   I was interested to see in an article by Mary Harris a discussion of women's work with numbers over the centuries: 'the making and buying and selling of everything that could be bought and sold and as we all know there is no-one more numerate than a market trader with a survival interest in the produce'. Renaissance manuals on domestic advice for women, she adds, expected them to be domestically numerate. She quotes from *The Book of Husbandry* (indeed!) by Sir Anthony Fitzherbert, in which the author lists the following duties of the wife: 'to go to market, to sell butter, cheese, milk, eggs, chickens, capons, hens, pigs, geese, and all manner of corn, and also to buy all manner of necessary things belonging to the household, and to make a true reckoning and account to her husband what she had received and what she hath paid' (Harris, 1997). It looks to me as if these women needed to be more skilled at mathematics than their men.

TB   This leads to the question of whether or not boys should have to learn mathematics up to the age of 16. Let's return to the aforementioned husband. He may be a school teacher of French, say, or a road sweeper, or a cabinet-maker. He relies on his wife to make domestic decisions and expects dinner on the table. If he asks a friend to tea, he expects all domestic arrangements to be altered to fit the new plan. He has no use for domestic mathematics. His is a different branch, yet he needs different skills.

ASW   Yes, and the public world – where he holds his job – is where power lies. The feminist writer Dale Spender has commented that, '"Mathematics" is part of the 99 per cent of the world's resources owned by men and they guard it well' (Spender, 1986). It reduces a girl's options if she doesn't have qualifications in mathematics. So many careers are closed to her otherwise.

It seems that in many ways, mathematics is still seen as a 'male' subject. At the post-compulsory level, there is still a large entry gap in favour of boys – and in physics, technology and economics, male dominance in terms of entry has actually increased (Arnot et al./OFSTED 1998). In one recent study, for example, it was found that 45 per cent of boys in the sample were studying mathematics at A level, compared with 22 per cent of girls (Cheng, Payne and Witherspoon, 1995).

TB   So what we're saying is that girls aren't really doing better at maths A level, because the only ones doing it are the ones likely to get the grades that will put them in line with the boys.

ASW   Exactly. And a possible reason for the gender gap in A level entry to mathematics is that although the percentage of boys and girls obtaining Grade C or above at GCSE is basically similar, boys actually perform better at the highest grades. In 1995, 7.4 per cent of girls taking maths at GCSE achieved A or A*, compared with 9.5 per cent of boys (Arnot et al./OFSTED 1998). One researcher's view is that 'the sex differences in A level mathematics entries are not surprising', as students may be expected to choose their A level subjects at least partly on the basis of expectation of success (Goulding, 1995).

So does this mean that boys are still doing better than girls? How does that relate to the old idea that women are inherently weaker at mathematics?

TB   It seems that this idea has been commonplace. If this is the case, it could be argued that things should be left up to what may indeed be naturally inherent. Or that it should be remedied by bringing them up to scratch with men, in the classroom.

ASW   Well at least a start has been made to make mathematics 'girl friendly'. In my school days, mathematics text books presented boys as problem-solvers – girls hardly featured at all and the questions were about cricket and cars. Here's an example based on cricket from a scholarship exam that was set for ten year olds in Peterborough in 1935: 'The lowest score made in an innings was 12. If this batsman had made 15, the average of the 11 for the innings would have been 31 exactly. What score did the side make?' (Written Arithmetic 2, County Examination, 1935).

But now it's different, isn't it? I remember that when you were taking your GCSE exam in mathematics, the questions went out of their way to highlight girls and also people of colour – so that it was boys, and especially white boys, who were in the background. Girls were often portrayed as cleverer than boys.

They look at a GCSE mathematics examination paper dated winter 1996, which reads: 'Darren estimates the probability of his passing a test at the first attempt at 0.6. If he fails he can take the test again. Using a tree diagram, or otherwise, calculate the probability that he will pass a) at the second attempt ... . Darren estimates the probability of his girlfriend passing the test at the first attempt as 0.8 ... .'

TB   But it seems to be different when you get to A level. I was skimming through a popular revision guide containing a coagulation of actual A level questions drawn from many examination boards' papers (Graham, Graham and Whitcombe, 1998). Contrary to my former belief, I became aware of the intrinsic sexism, which is hardly noticeable. Many questions are about 'a train driver', 'a biologist', or 'a water-skier', which seem quite neutral – a good idea in these times where it is safest to be as non-gender-specific as possible – until we come to the pronoun, which is almost invariably 'he'. There are just a few token female-orientated questions, which refer for example to 'Jane' or 'Susan, a biologist'.

ASW   It seems that deep-seated ideas about what makes for a 'successful working life' still divide along gender-related lines (Lightbody and Durndell, 1996). As before, it is overwhelmingly young men who choose to study engineering and mainstream science subjects at university.

TB   Actually that is a topical point. I recently attended an interview for entry to engineering at a top university. Out of about 30 people, there were only two girls, who instinctively gravitated together.

ASW   It sounds like nothing much has changed, then.

TB   It is now up to the new generation of school leavers to discover their own ways of dealing with these issues. And this book shows there is an opening for change, since 83 per cent of the authors are male. Perhaps a sequel will be brought out. Perhaps more than 10 per cent of its chapters will be from a female perspective – and perhaps that will reflect in a shift in national feeling.

6 Should mathematics be compulsory for all until the age of 16?

John White

Mathematics is a subject held in high esteem. It has traditionally occupied an unchallenged role within our culture. No other subject can match it in intellectual prestige. It is the hardest and most abstract of disciplines. Who could top a Cambridge wrangler?

According to research surveyed in a recent Qualifications and Curriculum Authority (QCA) review of curricular aims, 'parents, governors and employers all saw mathematics and English as the most important subjects' (QCA, 1998: 35). Is mathematics' high position in the academic pecking order justified? Are there good reasons to support it? In particular – and this is the main topic of this chapter – are there good reasons for its being compulsory from the age of five to 16?

Other chapters in this book examine different kinds of reasons for teaching and studying the subject, past and present. They can be divided into two broad groups, namely instrumental and non-instrumental. 'Instrumental' reasons – as I am using the term here (I realize it can have other uses) – are about the harnessing of mathematics to the demands of everyday life and of the economy. Non-instrumental ones are about other aims than these, for example about mathematics as a vehicle of mental training or as intrinsically interesting.

We need to assess these reasons insofar as they are still alive in current thinking. This is partly a matter of seeing whether the reasons will do at all – or whether there are intellectual or moral flaws in them which rule them out for anybody. But it is also partly a matter of examining the scope of the reasons which pass this first test – of seeing how far they are merely good reasons for some people in some circumstances, or whether they are powerful enough to justify compulsory mathematics for everybody up to the age of 16.

I

To start with non-instrumental reasons. The first task here is to separate the sound reasons from the dubious. Mathematical thinking has for millennia been closely associated with our unique nature as human beings. Both Plato and Descartes believed that the essence of the human is our ability to reason. Whereas emotions and desires belong to our bodies, we ourselves are only contingently associated with the latter and can continue to exist in their absence when the body dies. What we are essentially is souls or minds and the distinguishing feature of a soul or mind is that it engages in ratiocination. For both thinkers the highest type of reasoning is that furthest removed from anything to do with our bodily existence, that is, maximally abstracted from our ordinary social life as embodied creatures. For both of them, mathematical thinking occupies the highest rungs of the ladder, only to be superseded by philosophical reasoning in Plato's case and the certainty of the 'Cogito' in Descartes'.

It is from within this tradition that Fred Clarke, the eminent British educationalist who was Director of the Institute of Education between 1936 and 1945, wrote that 'the ultimate reason for teaching long division to little Johnny is that he is an immortal soul' (Clarke, 1923: 2). Few of us living in a more secular age could go along with the religious assumptions in this. Yet many more of us are insensibly influenced by other aspects of the Platonic-Cartesian theory. Especially the notion that mathematical thinking is in some way *superior* to other forms of thinking – both academic forms like those of the historian or literary critic, and the practical reasoning on which we rely day-to-day in the planning of our personal and institutional lives. In the Platonic-Cartesian tradition there was a reason why mathematical reasoning had this high status: its abstraction from the realities of embodied existence. Today we rightly take more seriously the fact of our embodiment: nearly all of us see ourselves not as minds which happen to be attached to bodies in this earthly life, but as sharing some bodily and some mental attributes with other animals and capable, owing to our linguistic capacities, of forms of social life not found in other species. Against this background there is no reason to elevate mathematical thinking above the many other sorts on which we depend, not least the practical reasoning mentioned above.

It is a myth, then, that if we want to develop young people's minds, one of the best ways of doing this is to give them a rigorous training in mathematics (see Peter Huckstep's comments on Sir Joshua Fitch, below). If we want them to act in the social world, there are better ways of equipping them mentally to do this than by making them adept in abstract operations which have least attachment to that world. In his *Republic* Plato made his philosopher kings study mathematics for ten years in early adulthood to help equip them for statesmanship. Yet despite the attractions of Plato's educational ideas for those responsible for elite education in Britain over the past 150 years, we have no reason to follow him in this. Getting into mathematics helps you, unsurprisingly, with mathematical reasoning, but there's no evidence that it makes you better at thinking about, say, history, current affairs or personal relationships.

Suppose we discard the mental training reason for learning mathematics? Are any other kinds of non-instrumental reason more convincing?

As Peter Huckstep shows below, Plato also held that studying mathematics gives us a direct insight into the structure of reality. In our own age, Bertrand Russell spent his early years exploring the foundations of mathematics in the belief that these would lead him towards the contemplation of eternal logical forms and a quasi-mystical sense of union with the universe (Monk, 1997: 159).

However, the idea that pure mathematics – on its own, not as handmaiden to science – is the key to understanding fundamental reality is now dead. Russell himself came to see his work as an exploration of language rather than the cosmos.

So far we have been looking at non-instrumental reasons that have proved to be failures. Are there others which are more successful?

II

I can think of three. The first is the intrinsic delight in mathematical thinking which many people have experienced and which Richard Smith has evoked so well. Part of this delight, especially in the upper reaches of the subject to do with matters such as pattern, simplicity and elegance of proof, has an aesthetic quality.

The second reason, not separable from the first, has to do with the necessary role of mathematics within science taken as intrinsically interesting in its own right apart from its technological applications.

The third reason, again inseparable from the first two, concerns the place of mathematics in our culture and, more generally, as a human achievement.

All three are good reasons in general why mathematics should be studied by some people. Yet this is where considerations of *scope* come into the picture. We are looking for good reasons why *everyone* should have to study mathematics until the age of 16. Do these three provide them?

At the very least, they do not show why mathematics should be privileged in the last Key Stage of the present National Curriculum in the way that it is. If we take the ten foundation subjects as our baseline, all of them are compulsory between the ages of 11 and 14, while between the ages of 14 and 16 mathematics, English, science, technology, physical education and a modern foreign language are compulsory and history, geography, music and art are not. In this scheme mathematics is privileged over these four non-compulsory subjects.

The first of the three good reasons for mathematics, about intrinsic delight, does not elevate mathematics above art and music, for these too provide this for some people. This point also undermines the second reason, as there is nothing to show that an interest in science for its own sake is privileged over an intrinsic interest in one of the arts or in history. The third reason, about the place of mathematics in our culture and as a human achievement, fails to show why mathematics should be privileged over history at Key Stage 4. Quite the reverse. This is because the reason only makes sense if the student has some kind of historical framework in which he or she can place cultural phenomena or great human achievements. I am assuming that history up to and including Key Stage 3 (age 14) does not provide enough of such a framework.

Perhaps we should abstract from current curricular arrangements in one country. Indeed, in the first version of the National Curriculum after 1988, *all* the foundation subjects were compulsory until the age of 16, so there was no issue then of privileging mathematics over the arts and history. Less parochially then, should all students be compelled to study mathematics from, say, the age of 11 to 16 for one or other of the three non-instrumental reasons?

The first reason for studying mathematics has to do with its intrinsic delights. No one would want to argue that a persisting love of mathematical thinking for its own sake is a *sine qua non* of any fulfilled life. A stronger argument would be that education should open every pupil's eyes to a number of *possible* intrinsic delights which they may or may not decide to take further as a major life commitment; and that mathematics, along with a range of other intrinsic goods, should be something to which everyone is exposed.

The argument is a powerful one in general; but not powerful enough, I think, to support compulsory mathematics for all until the age of 16. Three considerations speak against this: the need to prioritize within the school curriculum; children's inclinations; and the likely pattern of adult commitments.

On prioritizing: the general case for mathematics applies to a host of other activities, for example the arts, physical activities, chess, philosophy, physical science and anthropology. There is not space for all of these to be compulsory for all until the age of 16, so reasoned choices will have to be made.

On inclinations: by the age of 11 some children really take to mathematics as an intriguing subject in its own right, others do not. If those who lack inclination are compelled to persevere with the subject until the age of 16 in the hope that a taste for its non-instrumental aspects will develop, this may well be counterproductive for some, perhaps many, children, especially as they become attached to intrinsic delights in other areas.

On the likely pattern of adult commitments: common sense suggests that, however well-run and extensive any school courses in mathematics were, the proportion of adults who delighted in mathematical thinking for its own sake would be likely to be very small. Few would be willing to devote the time and effort required for such abstract and difficult activity. Human beings being what they are, most would prefer to spend any free time in their short lives on pleasures closer to the sensuous surface of life, for instance on those to do with relationships, sports and the arts. Common sense may be wrong about this, of course, and it would be interesting to see what evidence could be adduced to test it. One test would be to find out the proportion of mathematics graduates who continue to pursue the subject for intrinsic reasons as against those who abandon it in favour of other ends-in-themselves.

These considerations point towards a compulsory taster course in mathematics after the age of 11 rather than a compulsory five-year course. This would enable those who don't already have an inclination for it to see if one develops. If they find no hint of joy in it despite the taster course, it would be sensible to let them drop it. After all, there are plenty of alternatives among which they might find something more appealing. Beyond the taster courses, there would be voluntary courses, perhaps within some constrained option system, for those who like the subject. If teaching on the taster course has been sufficiently inspiring, one may expect many, perhaps most children to want to take the subject further, but it would be unrealistic to expect everyone to do so.

A word on the voluntary courses. There is every reason, given what we know of how people's intrinsic interests shift, why entry to these should be at any point, up to and indeed beyond the end of compulsory school-ing. School voluntary courses in mathematics and other subjects could be meshed into a wider system of further and adult education, with a right to opt in being available, and courses free of charge for younger people and some other groups.

The second non-instrumental reason is that a knowledge of mathematics is necessary for the pursuit of science for its own sake.

The three considerations of prioritizing, inclinations and likely pattern of adult commitment also apply to some extent to science, speaking against its being a compulsory subject for intrinsic reasons from the age of 11 to 16 (although there may be other reasons why it should be compulsory for this period). The combination of taster and voluntary courses in mathematics already referred to seems appropriate for both the first and second non-instrumental reasons described above.

I turn to the third of our non-instrumental reasons, to do with the place of mathematics in our culture and as a human achievement. I am excluding from this utilitarian reasons for mathematics to do with citizenship and the world of work, but will be looking at these in the third section of this chapter.

A leader from the *Daily Telegraph* (19 August 1998) about the award of the Fields Medal in mathematics to two British academics sets the scene. It begins:

> Mathematics is the master key to the Universe. Its mysteries may seem arcane to the layman, but without it we would still be living in a pre-scientific, pre-industrial world. Most educated people have little grasp of the arithmetic and geometry of the Ancient Greeks, yet none of their legacies has a more direct impact on our lives than those of Euclid, Archimedes or Diaphantos. As for the modern immortals, the great discoveries in physics of a Newton or an Einstein would have been impossible had they not also been superb mathematicians. Our society is shamefully ill-equipped to comprehend the mathematical mind.

I am sure all this is true. The only question is: does it provide a good reason for compulsory school courses in mathematics from the age of 11 to 16?

If it does, parallel arguments could be mounted for such pillars of our culture as philosophy, law and architecture. Should there then be five-year courses in all these subjects? (To say nothing of music, the visual arts, history and politics.)

Another issue is how much of the cultural importance of mathematics can one grasp from outside the subject? The *Daily Telegraph* leader communicates *something* of this to its readers, many, perhaps most, of whom probably know little mathematics. How much further could its account be filled out without requiring an insider's understanding of advanced mathematics?

Part of mathematics' cultural significance lies, as indicated in the excerpt, in its contribution to science. Many of those lacking a scientific education acquire some insight, often considerable insight, into the way the scientific advances of the last four centuries have radically transformed human life. They realize that many of these advances have depended on advanced mathematics, even though they lack an insider's knowledge of the latter.

In saying this, I am not, of course, claiming that mathematical knowledge adds nothing to one's appreciation of its cultural role. It surely deepens one's understanding considerably. The only issue, once again, is whether a five-year secondary course in mathematics is justified for cultural reasons. If one takes into account the considerations already mentioned about curriculum priorities and about children's inclinations, taster-plus-voluntary courses in mathematics with a cultural dimension to them seem the best answer.

III

I turn to the teaching and learning of mathematics for instrumental reasons, meaning by this its contribution to everyday life and to the world of work.

First, to sort out the good from the bad arguments. Elizabeth Anderson tells us that in nineteenth-century British universities:

> Students did learn some mathematics, although rarely at an advanced level. And math classes were valued more for the discipline and obedience they instilled through boring drill and rote exercises, than for their potential to sharpen students' analytical reasoning skills or to enable them to understand the basis of physical laws. (Anderson, 1998: 336)

There is no doubt, either, that discipline and obedience help to explain why arithmetic occupied so prominent a place in English elementary school codes from 1862 onwards. Richard Aldrich and David Crook (see

Chapter Three) have drawn our attention to the large amount of time spent on the subject and to endless practice sums that did not teach children anything new but kept their heads well down.

Obedience to orders and getting used to boring, mechanical tasks are personal characteristics tailor-made for the Work Culture of the nineteenth and earlier twentieth centuries. Schooling based on them treats pupils not as ends in themselves, but only as means to economic ends. I hope I can safely take it that this reason for teaching mathematics, usually arithmetic, can be ruled out on ethical grounds.

This leaves us with the sound instrumental reasons for studying mathematics.

(a) It is a commonplace that we all need some understanding of simple arithmetic to manage our personal finances, measure areas around the house, etc. How much we need, especially in the age of the calculator, is a further question. Even before calculators came on the scene, most adults had little cause to tap into their knowledge of long division or long multiplication or square roots.

(b) We also all need some mathematics from a civic point of view. We have to be able to think in terms of millions and billions in order to grasp anything of national housekeeping; we need to understand graphical and other representations of quantitative data on policy matters such as are found in the media; we need some insight into how such statistics can be misleadingly presented.

(c) Mathematics is also a *sine qua non* of very many jobs. (i) Sometimes the arithmetical knowledge already mentioned covers this, as in work on check-outs and simpler craft activities. (ii) More advanced mathematics is necessary for mathematics- and science-based jobs. (iii) Richard Noss, in his inaugural lecture (Noss, 1997), has also drawn attention to the 'hidden', unobvious, presence of mathematical thinking in various jobs. I will go into this further below.

There are three good reasons, therefore, (a), (b) and (c) for learning some mathematics. As before, the issue of scope now becomes salient. Do all these reasons apply to everybody? Insofar as they do, do they furnish a good reason for compulsory mathematics up to the age of 16?

(a) Most children can be expected to have mastered most of the basic arithmetic needed for everyday purposes by the end of primary schooling (age 11). There may have to be some remedial work for a few pupils, but beyond that a compulsory course for all would only have to cover a few areas not taught at primary level.

(b) Civic mathematics is important for everybody. There is a plain case for a short, focused compulsory course, preferably tied in with courses in education for citizenship.

(c) In discussing work-related mathematics, I shall use the same three categories, (i), (ii) and (iii) as above.

(i) The basic arithmetic required for many jobs will be largely acquired by the end of primary school.

(ii) Only a minority of students will be learning the advanced mathematics needed for mathematics- and science-based jobs. They will include those who show an early aptitude for the subject and want to do more of it, either for its own sake, or for what it leads on to, or both. They will opt for voluntary courses in non-basic mathematics in secondary schools. Other students may decide to take up mathematics later in the secondary school, or indeed after secondary school, having first become interested in some area of employment and then seen the necessity of advanced mathematics for that work. Voluntary courses would also be suitable for them.

There is a good case, based on the value of personal autonomy, for making sure that all secondary students have access to knowledge about the academic requirements for different jobs. These include mathematical requirements. It would be going too far compulsorily to equip all students early on with the academic requirements for a whole range of jobs, just in case they decided to choose one of these later. The first reason for this is that so many compulsory subjects would have to be included – not only advanced mathematics, but also criminal and civil law, geology, psychology, linguistics, Asian studies, etc. The second reason is that virtually all the compulsory studies would be vocationally useless for most students. Rather than thinking of pre-equipping students for vocational possibilities, we should ensure that they can take up voluntary courses in requisite subjects once their vocational preferences are clear.

(iii) We come back to Richard Noss's idea of the hidden presence of mathematics in many jobs: 'mathematics is not always visible, it lies beneath the surface of practices and cultures' (Noss, 1997: 5). He gives examples of nurses' use of a simple mathematical model of drug level; and of the growing use of computers in many jobs, where workers need to operate beyond a routine level : 'the massive computerization of systems ... will mean that more and more people will need to modify and rebuild systems with their own variables and parameters, not just plug in values to someone else's' (Noss, 1997: 17).

Given Noss's case, what implications does it have for the extent to which mathematics should be compulsory in secondary education? He does not explicitly draw any himself, but his call for a new conception of 'numeracy' which goes beyond basic arithmetical skills and equips people to understand the 'invisible' mathematics just described suggests that he *may* (?) think that all pupils should become numerate in this new sense.

Noss's own views on this aside, the case for a compulsory course for all does not seem to have been made. What proportion of the population will require the modelling and other job-related abilities that Noss mentions? We have no reason to think it is anywhere near 100 per cent. The further it falls short of this, the more pupils who are compulsorily inducted into this area of mathematics are learning something which will turn out to be useless to them. There is much more of a case for building this learning into voluntary courses which learners can choose to follow at any time from early secondary education onwards, including the time after they become attracted by career options which require this sort of mathematical attainment.

It is time to draw together the threads of the argument about acceptable instrumental reasons for studying mathematics. There is an unchallenge-able argument that all children should learn the basic mathematics, i.e. arithmetic, necessary for everyday life. This is a job almost exclusively for primary schools. If the current government's policies on numeracy succeed, by the year 2002 75 per cent of British children will have reached Level 4 in the area by the age of 11. That will provide them with the basic arithmetic they need to get by.

What role does that leave for the secondary school? None of the vocationally orientated arguments we looked at justify compulsory as distinct from voluntary classes. The only powerful case for compulsion concerns a short, focused course in civic mathematics.

IV

A little more thread-gathering. We have so far examined separately the non-instrumental and the instrumental reasons for studying mathematics and their curricular consequences. The instrumental arguments, as we have just seen, point to a compulsory basic course for all at primary level and a short course in civic mathematics somewhere in secondary education. The non-instrumental arguments suggest a taster course in mathematics for its own sake and for cultural reasons. At secondary level, the two proposals – instrumental and non-instrumental – taken together add up to a drastically reduced role for compulsory mathematics. At the same time, there would be a massively *increased* place at secondary level for voluntary courses, perhaps for various voluntary courses with different orientations, on the lines suggested by Richard Smith above.

I am far from advocating that compulsory curriculum time vacated by one subject should automatically be filled by other compulsory subjects. There is a general case for keeping compulsion down to the level at which it can be adequately justified. I say more on this below. However, if Steve Bramall (see Chapter Four) is right – as he surely is – that mathematics cannot give us insight into the ends of human life in the way that humanities subjects can (except, presumably, for the insight it can give us into the intrinsic features of mathematics), there is a strong case for letting more classes in compulsory literature, history, sociology and perhaps philosophy take up some of the slack.

One of the most intellectually courageous colleagues I have known in my time is Alan Hornsey, who before his retirement was Head of the Modern Languages Department at the Institute of Education. Alan has never wavered in his belief that the case for a compulsory modern language in the school curriculum had not been made. I know there are mathematics educators similarly sceptical of the conventional wisdom that mathematics should be compulsory for all 11 years of compulsory schooling. It would be good if their voices were heard more often.

Whatever stance mathematics educators take on this issue, I do not wish to imply that only those within mathematics education are authorities on how much and what mathematics should be compulsory. The issue is one for the citizen, not only the specialist. With the coming of the National Curriculum in 1988 this was recognized – in a way – via the *political* decision that mathematics should be compulsory from the age of 5 to 16. The trouble was that the political decision was not made on good enough grounds. After all, it was not only mathematics that was made compulsory for 11 years: the same was true for all but one of the other foundation subjects. This fact alone should be enough to cast doubt on the well-foundedness of the government's decision, for if that decision *had been* well-founded, what a coincidence it would have been that pros and cons about the length of compulsory courses in art, science, English, technology, history, music, geography and physical education were resolved in each case in exactly the same way to produce the 11-year recommendation. Surely, one is inclined to think, a careful review of the arguments would have led to very different proposals for the different subject areas.

The extent to which children are compelled to attend school classes is no trivial matter. In the adult world we rightly refrain as far as possible from compelling other people to do things. True, people are obliged to pay income tax, go to prison for certain offences and drive on the left. However, good reasons have to be provided for such compulsion: we do not see it as an arbitrary matter. We should take the same stance towards children at school. The system should not arbitrarily oblige them to do this course or that. There have to be good reasons why constraint has to be used. There is no doubt in my own mind that such good reasons are available in many, many cases. I am not suggesting at all that children should be at liberty to do – or not do – whichever courses they want. There is nothing to be said in favour of such an ideological stance. I am calling, instead, for the piecemeal, careful examination of arguments, most of which are likely to differ from subject to subject.

It may be that, in the case of mathematics education, such judicious investigation will come up with a copper-bottomed argument for compulsory mathematics for all from the age of 5 to 16. I promise you, I will believe it when I see it.

7 Mathematics as a vehicle for 'mental training'

Peter Huckstep

What is the purpose of learning mathematics? What is it is for? Or, more pointedly, why must we learn it? One immediate response to such questions is simply to point out that mathematics is *useful*. Indeed, the two questions 'Why learn x?' and 'What is the use of x?', although not identical in meaning, are nonetheless somewhat interchangeable in uncritical discourse. So to assert the usefulness of mathematics as its justification rather leaves things as they are. Of course, we could underline this first response by presenting a catalogue of the various ways in which the subject is useful. For example, it seems hardly possible to gainsay the usefulness of some elementary mathematics. The value of counting and the carrying out of simple numerical operations, at the very least, is impossible to deny. Without them we would all be severely limited in our daily lives. The progress of civilization, too, is testimony to the usefulness of more advanced topics in mathematics. However, between the rudimentary and the advanced lie those topics that many pupils and even reflective adults sometimes find hard to value.

It is at this point that a divergence exists between the uses to which mathematics can be put, and the uses that everyone might reasonably make of mathematics. To perceive such a divergence leads one to suppose that the usefulness of mathematics does not sufficiently justify the prolonged learning of the subject in compulsory education. One solution to this problem is to seek suitable non-utility reasons for learning mathematics.

Thus, it is sometimes suggested that mathematics should be studied, largely for its own sake. Whilst it is possible to provide some justification for studying the subject for sheer enjoyment (Cockcroft, 1982; Wells, 1989), this is not the rationale that will be discussed here. The notion of usefulness is a broad notion (Huckstep, 1999) and deserves to be pursued a little further.

When the usefulness of mathematics has been in question (Hardy, 1967; Whitcombe, 1988; Davis, 1995; Andrews, 1998), it is often a particular kind of usefulness – practical usefulness – that is intended. Precisely what is meant by 'practical usefulness' is not absolutely clear, but let us suppose that it at least implies the application of mathematical knowledge to achieve fairly immediate and accessible extra-mathematical ends in everyday life, by the possessor of such knowledge. Practical usefulness thus conceived makes way for a rather different goal for mathematics: its use (if it must even be called 'use') by an educator, for the purpose of 'mental training'. Roughly, then, a helpful distinction between two important senses of usefulness may be made by viewing mathematics either as a *tool* or as a *vehicle*. It is to an examination of the latter view – mathematics as a vehicle for mental training – that we now turn.

Although the claim that mathematics trains the mind has often been rejected, particularly during the last century, it remains an idea that dies hard. It has had a long history that dates back to Ancient Greece. Moreover, mental training of some kind or other has often been valued more highly than the practical usefulness of the subject. This is true both of statements in antiquity, and in more modern times, particularly in the last two or three centuries. Writers of professional handbooks and reports still endorse the view. For example, in its *Mathematics 5 to 11: A Handbook of Suggestions* HMI wrote:

> Mathematics can provide a valuable mental training, but many other things can do this just as well; and mathematics cannot be justified on this ground alone if it deteriorates into stereotyped working to rule, with the higher functions of the mind neglected. Mathematics can be justified as a *training for the mind*, but the training also needs to serve other purposes which can be understood by the pupil at the time. There

is something wrong with the teaching if the reply to 'Why are we learning this?' has to be 'You will understand later on!'

(HMI, 1979: 4–5, emphasis added)

Clearly, this endorsement comes with a warning. Mathematics is by no
means the sole vehicle of such training, nor the most suitable. It is not the
sole justification for learning it either. Certain conditions must also hold:
training as mere drill is ruled out and the development of the 'higher
functions of the mind' is deemed to be essential. In addition, fairly immediate returns are also expected of such training.

But what does mental training consist in? It would be scarcely helpful,
and is indeed circular, to try to justify mathematics by suggesting that
mental training takes place simply through the acquisition of mathematical
knowledge. Of course, in learning anything the capacity of the mind is
extended and training invariably involves the acquisition of knowledge.
Trained historians, philosophers and surgeons are all trained partly in
respect of knowledge that they have acquired. So it might be argued that
in studying mathematics one is inescapably undergoing mental training
of some kind. Put like this, however, it begs the question with which we
began: why must we receive *this* training?

The philosophic model

Self-mastery

Leaving aside mathematics for the moment, there is one notion of mental
training that specifically addresses, and changes for the better, some
natural tendency of the mind. This much is clear in what William James
(1981 edn) wrote in *The Principles of Psychology*:

> The faculty of voluntarily bringing back a wandering attention over and
> over again is the very root of judgment, character and will. No one is
> *compos sui* if he have it not. An education which should improve this
> faculty would be the education par excellence. (James, 1981: 401)

James is reiterating a belief, particularly popular in the nineteenth century,
that the faculty of attention can be improved by training. Here, in distinction

from the acquisition of mere knowledge, mental training promotes a kind of *self-mastery*; mastery over the tendency to lose attention. Yet although such self-mastery could, in terms of educational aims be viewed as part of autonomy, attention-training, although surely desirable, is no longer fashionable as an educational aim.

Nevertheless, outside education within the context of mental health, certain forms of stress-relief do involve training the attention by *meditation*. This involves being consciously aware of the familiar tendency of the attention to flit involuntarily from one object to another; then, by focusing on a designated object of thought or perception, repeatedly and patiently regaining the attention whenever it strays. The fruits of such sustained attempts at concentration are supposed to include calmness and presence of mind. Self-mastery of this kind, then, contributes to human well-being in a special way. Many advocates would claim much more, but all that is sought here is a process that exemplifies a clear and valuable case of mental training. Meditation lies outside the sustained and systematic learning of formal education as it largely involves what educationists would call mere drill. However, one way of showing how mathematics might provide mental training, would be to explain how it provides self-mastery of a similar kind through *cognition*, and thus within the usual sphere of education.

The need for meditation arises from a certain mental disquiet, but there has been a dominant strand of human thought in which it is acknowledged that a similar and natural condition exists and is one which education can alleviate. It has often been suggested that there is a potential conflict between reason and passion (or appetite) in the human psyche. A lack of self-mastery in this respect is conveyed by the commonplace remark of 'the heart ruling the head'. One of the earliest theories of education in which the fundamental role of education consists of providing self-mastery of this kind derives from Plato (1955 edn) in *The Republic*. Plato attempted to show how philosophic reflection upon the nature of mathematics can lead to human well-being in a way not dissimilar to that claimed by advocates of meditation – a state of peace and calmness. It may seem rather strange that mathematics can be a means to a state of bliss! But the training that Plato had in mind was not simply a quick fix. It involved a long process of seeking out the very source of Reason, which, once reached, would guarantee a vision of life free from the demands that the appetites make upon us.

One difficulty with Plato's philosophic model of mental training is that it rests upon his own distinctive metaphysics which would be unlikely to persuade the modern mind. Reason, for Plato, was a kind of acquaintance with its *source* – the super-sensible Forms – from which everything was supposed to derive its meaning and order. Self-mastery was ultimately achieved by living a life ruled by reason. However, Plato's role for mathematics can still be explained, to some extent, independently of the belief in the existence of such reified reason. With or without his metaphysics we can understand what Plato had in mind by swallowing, if only momentarily, the rather quaint way in which he thought mathematics provided especially significant 'paradoxes', which were less prominent in other areas of learning. Such 'paradoxes' are supposed to stir the mind into action and provide a stimulus for philosophizing. It seemed to him, for example, that what we would now call the 'concept of one' cannot in a sense be abstracted from instances of single objects, as every object is simultaneously a single entity and consists of many parts. So it seems we cannot isolate unity in perception, as it is always combined with plurality. Once we reflect upon this state of affairs, Plato thought that we must find ourselves questioning the origins of our number concepts. In so doing, he believed that we begin our journey towards apprehending the source of Reason.

Self-knowledge

Outside education the paradoxes of Plato have been very influential, but recently Davis (1995) has revived an interest in strikingly similar situations, which he uses to construct a non-utility rationale for the learning of mathematics. Just as Plato was struck by the fact that all objects of sense are both single and not single, Davis is similarly impressed by what we might call the 'unsayable' in mathematics. From a transcript of a classroom episode, he focuses on the remark of a pupil, Jiema, who appears to permit degrees of equivalence in fractions. Jiema asserts that $\frac{3}{9}$ is not as equivalent to $\frac{2}{6}$ as certain other fractions are, in particular $\frac{1}{3}$ and $\frac{4}{12}$. Davis interprets this response in a novel way. He welcomes it as being at odds with the strictly categorical way in which mathematical and logical propositions have been traditionally viewed. In this respect, one fraction either is, or, is not equivalent to another; there are no intermediate states. Davis himself does not believe that there should be degrees of equivalence, only that the unorthodox nature of Jiema's assertion somehow throws the whole question of strict categorical ways of thinking back at us.

In *The Republic* Plato reflects upon a state of affairs closely related to the one that Davis discusses. It, too, seems to be unsayable because it flies in the face of the categorical way in which we often speak. A persistent and articulate Jiema speaking to her fellow classmate might equally have said something like the following:

> 'And what about the many things which are double something else? If they are double one thing can't they be equally well regarded as half something else?' 'Yes.' 'And things which we say are large or small, light or heavy, may equally well be given the opposite epithet.' 'Yes, they may be given both.' 'Then can we say that any of these many things *is*, any more than it *is not* what anybody says it is?'
>
> (Plato, 1955 edn: 274–275)

Whilst Plato and Davis have similar starting points, it is where the ambivalence expressed in their examples lead to that distinguishes the two theorists. Plato thought that the only candidates for knowledge were those objects that *are*. Of the objects remaining, some, he thought, are only *becoming*, and therefore can only be sources of belief (or opinion). Any other supposed objects *are not* and hence are sources of error or ignorance. Clearly, nowadays we would argue that Plato was conflating the distinct uses that 'are' and 'is' have in both existence and in predication. Nevertheless, what is important is Plato's conclusion that many things – in particular the objects of sense perception – are only becoming and, as such, cannot constitute knowledge. In short, the world which we perceive is not reality.

However, as it was knowledge that Plato sought, he assumed that this must lie outside sense perception and, therefore, that there must be an independent world of Forms. Education, he thought, partly consisted in shaking us out of the complacent state in which we take for granted that the perceived world is reality. It entailed our turning towards the Forms. The revelation of paradoxes of the kind in the extract above – where things appear to be and not to be – was supposed to raise the central question of what exists and, hence, what could be known. For Plato, Jiema's remarks about fractions would be showing the same kind of thing. As mathematics provides an ideal vehicle for such revelations, Plato believed that it provided the origins of a revised understanding of what reality must be. Therefore, we could quite rightly say that Plato would agree with Davis that even elementary mathematics topics 'offer a rich ground for exploring what tends to be taken-for-granted' (Davis, 1995: 6).

As I have already remarked, few, if any, would accept Plato's metaphysical picture of reality. So there are notable differences between the ancient theory of Plato and the contemporary view of Davis. What Davis believes we take for granted, and which he thinks mathematics offers a rich ground for exploring, is not our assumption that perception constitutes reality. He is urging us to somehow look *within* perception rather than *beyond* it. Davis is concerned with the mathematical basis of that perception, not its validity as a source of knowledge. He insists that mathematics is ubiquitous in perception and does not want to challenge the status of that perception. He is not suggesting, like Plato, that we should eschew the value of sense perception in favour of some ultimate reality. For Davis, it seems to be the nature of mathematical assumptions that are at issue. They are in principle always subject to revision, as the discovery of alternative consistent geometries has shown conclusively.

What is not clear, however, is the extent to which a pupil can, and needs to, take part in the revision of mathematical assumptions. Stripped of the metaphysical background of the ancient thinker, Jiema's remarks do not seem to have quite the same kind of force in Davis's theory as they would in Plato's. It seems that Davis is suggesting that an important purpose of mathematics lies in its being a vehicle for a special kind of self-knowledge. However, he prefers to look at such instances as Jiema's remarks not so much as a revelation but as something which challenges. All the same, what is challenged is, he says, 'Not only what we know and believe, but who we are'. Whether or not this may be characterized as self-knowledge, one thing is clear: the inwardness invoked in this remark certainly distinguishes his conclusions from those of Plato.

One way, then, of becoming clearer about the notion of mental training endorsed in The HMI 'handbook', discussed above, is to suppose that some kind of reflective or philosophic model is implied. However, whilst the philosophic model does fulfil the development of important 'higher functions' of the mind, it is still not clear that the goals of such a training provides the kind of immediacy also required in the document.

The HMI handbook is not, however, the only case made for mental training in recent years. *Mathematics Counts* (Cockroft, 1982) also suggests, in a rather more muted way, that mathematics can be justified as a form of mental training, more explicitly by developing 'powers of logical thinking, accuracy and spatial awareness' (Cockroft, 1982: 2). The Report goes on to reiterate the cautionary remarks of the earlier document, noting that it 'depends upon the way in which mathematics is taught' and also that 'the study of a number of other subjects can develop these powers as well'. Whether or not 'accuracy' *per se*, rather than accuracy in mathematics, can be improved by learning mathematics is questionable. The same seems to be true of 'spatial awareness', although this is often an assumption that teachers make from time to time in teaching 'shape and space'.

The belief that 'logical thinking' is developed through mathematics has certainly been an established view, but whilst mathematics is surely a logical discipline the extent to which it presupposes a logical mind, rather than produces one, is a nice point. Yet the introductory paragraph of the Programmes of Study in the revised National Curriculum in England (Department for Education and Employment/Qualifications and Curriculum Authority, 1999) is less cautious. In setting out 'the importance of mathematics' it asserts that 'Mathematics equips pupils with a uniquely powerful set of tools to understand and change the world. These tools include *logical reasoning*, problem-solving skills, and the ability to think in abstract ways' (Department For Education and Employment/Qualifications and Curriculum Authority, 1999: 6; emphasis added).

Admittedly, there is little here to suggest that mathematics is a 'vehicle' for the educator rather than a tool for the pupil, but it is upon the question of the generality of 'logical reasoning' that much still hangs. Games like chess involve logical reasoning but we do not single these out for special consideration on the curriculum, as they embody what have been called 'narrow capacities' (Passmore, 1980: 52). Historically, reasoning *procedures* (qualified or not by 'logical') have had a special attraction. Moreover, it has often been supposed that the development of these procedures constitutes a form of mental training for which mathematics is the ideal vehicle. It is this view which will now be examined in more detail.

The procedural model

Although logic has traditionally always been part of the subject-matter of philosophy, the teaching of the subject which for some has been regarded as the very science of inference is not an explicit part of the curriculum for compulsory schooling in England. Logic usually arises only as part of mathematical education rather as ethics might arise as part of religious education. Some educational manuals make specific use of 'logical' apparatus and tasks are given to pupils with the intention of developing logical thinking. These tasks are supposed to promote an awareness of the 'logical constants' of negation, conjunction, disjunction and implication by such activities as sorting which make pivotal use of such words as 'not', 'and' 'or' and 'if ... then'. Yet although mathematics makes use of this 'logic', it is seldom taught in such a self-conscious way.

Nevertheless, the axiomatic nature of mathematics – the deriving of mathematical conclusions by strict rules of passage from certain ultimate premises believed to be true of the extra-mathematical world – was precisely what has made it a discipline of the highest prestige since the time of Euclid. Euclidean geometry for centuries was (wrongly) supposed to offer truths about the actual space in which we live. This was still true much later, in the seventeenth century when Descartes gave mathematical method a special place in his *Rules for the Direction of the Mind*. However, it was not only the guarantee of substantive truths of the extra-mathematical world that Descartes believed the procedures embodied, but also the simplicity and self-evident nature of the mathematical premises and inferences involved in deductions. He believed that these processes, of the 'Universal Mathematics', were the essence of wisdom for every individual, not simply 'for the purpose of resolving this or that difficulty of scholastic type, but in order that his understanding may light his will to its proper choice *in all the contingencies of life*' (Descartes, 1969 edn: 37; emphasis added).

Descartes seems to have written little or nothing explicitly about education, even though his account of wisdom, if true, has important implications for educators. It remained for others to develop more explicit theories of education which urge the value of mathematical processes as a vehicle for the educator.

A more developed view, which runs along similar lines to Descartes', was set out by Sir Joshua Fitch, an inspector of training colleges during the latter part of the nineteenth century. For Fitch, mathematical reasoning was the most important 'object' in learning mathematics. In his *Lectures on Teaching* given at Cambridge at the turn of the nineteenth century, he remarked that 'the fundamental reason for teaching mathematics is because a certain kind of mental exercise, of unquestioned service in connection with *all conceivable subjects of thought*, is best to be had in the domain of mathematics' (Fitch, 1902: 342; emphasis added).

Clearly the (questionable) assumption that mathematical processes are of general application is one upon which the value of such processes rides. (Notice that for Descartes these processes were applicable to 'all the contingencies of life' and Fitch similarly asserts that they apply to 'all conceivable subjects of thought'.) It is this very assumption that makes the acquisition of such processes such a pressing reason to learn mathematics.

Fitch's argument appeals to a view which still, rightly, has much support, namely that the learning of all subjects should not be simply a matter of learning isolated facts, but rather the derivation of those facts from principles. It might be helpful to view Fitch's claim as a generalization across all the subject areas of an important aspect found in the current emphasis on mental mathematics. It is that mental mathematics should consist not solely of the recall of 'known facts' but additionally involve the figuring out of 'derived facts' by the application of a range of 'mental strategies' (Askew, 1977).

Fitch acknowledges that both inductive and deductive inferences are at work in the various disciplines, but in the end he favours the pursuit of the latter. Furthermore, as he views mathematics as largely articulated by deductive inferences, he concludes that the most important justification for mathematics is its use as a particular kind of mental training. As he puts it, 'the proper office of arithmetic is to serve as elementary training in logic' (Fitch, 1902: 321).

Fitch embraced a view of knowledge as a body of propositions articulated by principles the inferences from which mathematics was particularly well placed to serve. However, this thoroughgoing reliance on the role of principles in *all* knowledge has been criticized by various contemporary writers. Passmore, for example, has pointed out that:

> There is no principle from which it can be deduced that Henry VIII broke with the Church of Rome, or how rapidly the population of India is increasing, or how many ribs a human being has, or when President Kennedy was assassinated, or how distant the moon is from the earth, or, even, that chloroform is an anaesthetic or that platypuses suckle their young. (Passmore, 1980: 97)

Hamlyn (1967) makes the same point. He agrees that explanatory theories, as in the sciences, have general laws from which deduction of facts may be made. But he remarks that 'it is difficult to see how large parts of history or literature could be said to have a structure in this sense' (Hamlyn, 1967: 29). Hamlyn insists that in learning there must always be a 'delicate balance between principles and cases'. Thus, in distinguishing between different kinds of disciplines it is clear that not all of them are articulated by principles of the kind that mathematical reasoning could serve.

A more sustained and penetrating criticism of the faith in what he calls 'idealised logic' can be found in the work of Toulmin (1958). One of Toulmin's aims in his book *The Uses of Argument* is to reveal two models of reasoning: one based on the procedures of jurisprudence and the other based on formal logic that has mathematics as its model. One of the main points of Toulmin's argument is the nowadays fairly established view that discourse takes place in a variety of non-reducible contexts. Often influenced by Wittgenstein, several theorists have insisted that there are different kinds of discourse and hence irreducible kinds of knowledge and facts. In education, for example, Hirst (1965) has famously attempted to delimit kinds of knowledge on the basis of their distinctive concepts and methods of validation. More recently, some of the theorists of the 'critical thinking' movement have also been quick to deny the existence of general powers of thought. Nevertheless, the issue, as I have already remarked, dies hard. Toulmin's distinction between mathematical reasoning and that found in jurisprudence has been somewhat side-stepped by the prominent mathematician and writer Morris Kline (1972), who uses the context of law precisely for the task of elucidating the axiomatic method in action outside explicitly mathematical contexts. Also the theory of distinct 'Forms of Knowledge' has been challenged on the grounds that the existence of the Forms themselves is evidence of certain general mental powers (Elliott, 1975).

A more modest view: mathematics as an initiation into reasoning

It is interesting to note that a sceptical view on the scope of mathematical processes across the various 'contingencies of life', 'subjects of thought' or whatever writers have thought such processes could possibly range over, is by no means a recent one. Some 50 years before Fitch gave his lectures, Thomas Tate in his influential book *The Philosophy of Education*, defended a more cautious view of mathematics as a vehicle for mental training. He wrote:

> Although the mathematical sciences may form one of the best initiatory trainings of the reasoning powers ... it only exercises the mind in appreciating one kind of evidence – namely, *mathematical evidence*. Some other subject, therefore, should be adopted for the purpose of developing the reasoning powers of children in relation to *moral evidence*. (Tate, 1854: 90)

For Tate, the cultivation of reason 'in a well-regulated mind, holds the *mastery* of all the other faculties: it gives strength and precision to every one of them, and harmonizes and regulates their operations as a whole' (Tate, 1854: 88; emphasis added). There are, here, some echoes of Plato's view of the mind as involving parts or faculties, which have a tendency to conflict and are in need of harmonization, yet, whilst some mention is made of the passions, Tate prefers to contrast reason with imagination. Thus, the cultivation of reason is supposed to prevent us from becoming 'the victims of sophistry, or the willing slaves of superstition and bigotry' (Tate, 1854: 88).

Tate asserts that 'the reasoning powers of a child are exercised whenever we put the question *why*, or receive the answer *because*'. His requirement here is modest. He seems less concerned than Plato and Descartes with finding or constructing the *source* of reason from mathematics but more with its *modus operandi*. For Tate, the reasoning faculty develops in the first instance as pupils begin to make correct inferences and understand the necessity of responding appropriately to questions.

The same characteristics of mathematics that so impressed Descartes and Fitch – simplicity, clarity and certainty – are drawn out by Tate to show why mathematics is such an ideal vehicle for developing the reasoning powers:

1. Nothing is taken for granted or on mere authority; for its principles of reasoning are axioms or self-evident truths.

2. Its proper objects are the relations of numbers, lines and spaces, things which are cognizable by our senses, and which can be defined and measured, with a precision of which the objects of no other kinds of reasoning are susceptible. (Tate, 1854: 80)

In contrast to this, Tate suggests that reason and argument outside mathematics require different backing which is often not only less accessible, but also of a kind that relies upon authority. However, despite being a particularly helpful exemplification of how reason-giving is essential in a range of areas of life, mathematics has little or nothing to show about the particular kinds of reasons that are appropriate elsewhere. However, it can help us to realize that reasons *of some kind* will be appropriate there. In learning to engage in mathematical reasoning, then, we come to learn to value reason-giving *in general*, and become disposed to seek and supply reasons.

Tate gives a wealth of examples of reasoning in several different categories, illustrating inferences that can be made from general statements. Moreover, these inferences follow from statements the backing and warrant for which are clearly based on authority. In the following example, the truth of the premise is not self-evident: 'Misery, disease, and death always follow drunkenness, dissipation, and all such crimes: then vice and misery are inseparably connected' (Tate, 1854: 96).

However, from this example a mathematical one may be constructed which relies upon more accessible evidence as its backing: 'A whole number whose last digit is a zero is divisible by 5: then 166340 is divisible by 5'. However, when we compare other of Tate's examples with a mathematical one of our own, things are not quite so convincing. Compare, for example: 'All animals with four feet are called quadrupeds: then, a cow must be a quadruped. A fowl is not a quadruped – why?' (Tate, 1854: 93) with: 'All quadrilaterals that have four right angles are called rectangles: then a square must be a rectangle. Not all parallelograms are rectangles – why?' Clearly, the backing for the conclusion 'a cow must be a quadruped' is based on the authoritative statement about what is meant by 'quadruped'. However, the mathematical argument is also based on the 'authority' of the use of words such as 'quadrilateral' and 'parallelogram' in precisely the same way. But leaving aside the authority involved in clarifying the meaning of a word, rather than authority of a more widespread kind, Tate does seem to have a point where elementary mathematics is concerned. We can certainly see for ourselves the truth of such mathematical propositions as 'Every number that is divisible by 10 is divisible by 5' and we can make reasoned conclusions from such premises.

Nevertheless, it is worth considering whether or not other activities can equally provide the same purpose for which Tate believed that mathematics was such an ideal vehicle. Tate himself singles out History as a subject which can also cultivate the reasoning powers when rightly taught. One might also suppose that certain games like chess may similarly exemplify rational procedures, except perhaps that players are not normally called upon to explain their strategies. It is in respect, where discourse is essential to the activity, that mathematics does seem to have a special place that is fairly resistant to objections and alternatives.

Even in everyday life opportunities arise for asking 'Why?' and eliciting responses beginning with 'because'. Whilst much of the evidence appealed to in such familiar settings is arguably based on authority, some reasoning is surely based upon backing which depends upon fairly straightforward perceptual evidence. For example, such reasoning as 'Why are you taking off your coat?' 'Because I'm hot' seems to be based on evidence that is perfectly clear and direct. Indeed Tate does make it clear that 'before children are taught any systematic course of study, they should be led to reason about common things, facts and events' (Tate, 1854: 92). However, he still upholds mathematics as being of special importance claiming that 'the earliest conceptions of a child relate to form and number, and they are the first which their minds are capable of viewing abstractedly'. So it seems that elementary mathematics provides a simple and fairly self-contained system of results which are missing in everyday situations and in which more sustained explanation may be sought on behalf of the pupil. However, the attractiveness of Tate's account still depends upon a sensitive trade-off between those aspects of his theory which distinguish it from the ambitious claims of earlier procedural accounts, and those which distinguish it from the value of reason in familiar contexts like games and the utterances found in everyday life.

Tate's account sits well with the demands of recent policy documents. As far as the HMI's *Handbook of Suggestions* discussed above is concerned, his modest view of mental training involves the application of intelligence –not mere drill – and arguably has fairly immediate effects, too. To some extent, it is also reflected in the current metacognitive approaches in the National Numeracy Strategy where, amongst other things, pupils are encouraged to 'explain their methods and reasoning using correct mathematical terms' (Department for Education and Employment, 1998: 12). It does, therefore, appear to be a particularly convincing account.

Conclusions

This critical review of certain dominant models of mental training has been carried out to see whether a justification for learning mathematics can be found which does not appeal to practical utility. However, the most plausible account of mental training suggests that it applies particularly to the *elementary* stages of mathematics learning. Indeed, what has been called here the 'modest' view of mental training is valued precisely because it provides an early initiation into rational behaviour. If we delay this process, then the other disciplines must take care of themselves. So a mental training rationale for learning mathematics does arise, but at a stage when the force of practical utility arguments is at its strongest, and where supplementary justification is scarcely necessary. The same point can be made when considering the alternative model of mental training where mathematics is supposed to provide stimulation for reflective thinking. For Plato, such reflection depended upon a mature approach to the subject, yet it is in the elementary areas of mathematics that this typically takes place. Few convincing reasons are given by Plato, or recently by Davis, for sustained learning in complex areas of mathematics for this purpose.

What has been presented here is, of course, highly selective, but the models discussed represent some of the clearest and most persuasive accounts which have been presented throughout history and upon which many of our assumptions have been based. By closely connecting these models to the sketchy remarks on the topic found in recent policy documents, we can see that justifications in terms of mental training are, paradoxically, strongest where they are least needed, i.e. at the elementary stage of learning the subject, where the practical utility justification is at its most incontrovertible.

8 Why must mathematics be a statutory part of the secondary curriculum for all?

Eric Blaire

The key debate that occurs in schools, homes and universities is at what point should young people stop having to study mathematics and not whether they should study it at all. The line I take in this chapter is that mathematics should be studied for as long as a pupil or student is compelled to be in school or college. This is not to argue that for all that time everyone is 'doing so many periods of mathematics' each week. There is not space here to argue in detail about the limitations of an integrated or an interdisciplinary approach to the curriculum, but it should not be assumed that at Key Stage 4 mathematics has to be developed either solely or mainly as a separate subject. This chapter does not consider why parents, teachers, pupils and governors expect mathematics to be a core curriculum area at least throughout primary education, but assumes that for a variety of instrumental and non-instrumental reasons this is taken to be so. Hopefully, the arguments presented here, for the continued presence of mathematics beyond the age of 11, would justify the place of mathematics in the primary curriculum too. This argument will go beyond either of the lines presented by John White (see Chapter Six) for instrumental and non-instrumental justifications. He gives the 'instrumental justification' as 'harnessing of mathematics to the demands of everyday life and of the economy. Non-instrumental ones are about other aims than these, for example about mathematics as a vehicle of mental training or as intrinsically interesting'. The line of argument taken in this chapter brings the instrumental and non-instrumental justifications together, for mathematics is seen as both a mental activity, 'the science of possibilities' involving disciplined imagination, and simultaneously as providing models for everyday life discussions, both in the natural and social sciences.

Many people would want to see the end of compulsion at the age of 14. They would argue that once pupils can choose among the range of subjects they have experienced up to then, they should have freedom to choose or to drop any subjects, probably excepting English, but including mathematics. The kind of argument presented is that mathematics is no more important for everyday life than history. There is also the valid argument that compulsion can be counterproductive. However, this line could be taken at Key Stage 3 or earlier. Education is not necessarily linked to flexibility, but is linked to well-reasoned choice.

John White argues that when options begin, say at the age of 14:

> School voluntary courses in mathematics and other subjects could be meshed into a wider system of further and adult education, with a right to opt in being available, and courses free of charge for younger people and some other groups.

Part of this kind of argument is that there is little more to be covered than that reached by age eleven that is crucial to everyday life. There may be a bit more, but that is needed for interpretation and can be covered in civics or the like, so the argument runs. Along with this can be the optional courses for those taking a particular vocational pathway. John White argues that this provides a sufficient curriculum for healthy educational progress for all.

What critics of the present system such as John White miss is that mathematics is not to be characterized by content, but rather by the illuminating processes that it accesses. There is something special about cutting young people off from mathematics that is logically different from cutting them off from any other subject. Chris Ormell identifies mathematics as a 'modelling system'. It helps one to look at possibilities in all situations and not just mathematical ones. There is more to mathematics than a technique to help one improve one's thinking skills. This mathematics applicable approach is predicated on the belief that imagination and identification are powerful vehicles for education in mathematics. Pupils are effectively motivated by being given the opportunity to tackle context-related problems that require them to generate models of what could possibly happen and possible solutions. The most famous context problem generated by the members who later formed the Mathematics Applicable Group (MAG) was about informing people waiting at a bus stop when the next bus would come along. This problem was set in the context of the School Council Sixth Form Applicable Mathematics Curriculum Project in about 1970 and I now pass such bus stops every day on the Uxbridge Road. The problem was reproduced as a booklet by the MAG in 1979, entitled *The Electronic Bus Stop*, still almost 20 years before the real bus stop was on the streets. The key point that Ormell (1996) has expressed many times is that mathematics provides 'priceless foresight ... when fully assimilated into an informed, positive and realistic point of view'.

If one accepts the Ormell approach, then the following line by John White is not correct:

> Getting into mathematics helps you – unsurprisingly – with mathematical reasoning, but there's no evidence that it makes you better at thinking about, say, history, current affairs or personal relationships.

John White misses the point that mathematics does make you better able to think through arguments in history or current affairs, and even, if one can be at times emotionally detached, in personal relationships. It provides the technique for considering possibilities and that is unique.

Steve Bramall (see Chapter Four) also falters in his line of argument. It is essentially naive, in being based on a particular conception of mathematics as language, without any reference to mathematics as the science of possibilities. It is this and not the fact that it can be seen as another language, that gives mathematics the uniqueness that requires its central place and permanent state in the balloon debate to which Bramall refers. It is the disciplined imagining of mathematics that provides the special form of thinking that pupils need developed as long as possible. The age of 16 is an arbitrary cut-off point, determined by the fact that in this country it is the point at which compulsory education for all, ends. If that age were ten or 20, then those would be the ages to which mathematics would rightly be compulsorily taught.

One can agree with Bramall that mathematics is to be seen as 'a means of saying things about the world, or an aspect of the world, that is unique and powerful'. Bramall misses the point that mathematics says things about an infinite number of possible worlds and nothing else can do that. The fact that social sciences including sociology are invaluable does not refute the argument that mathematics, recognized as the science of possi-bilities, is essential to understanding elsewhere. Mathematical possibilities are applicable to natural or social sciences. Those cut off from mathematics too early are left without the skills to conjecture in this way. This limits their scientific development and understanding of the world and possible worlds, whether in the natural or social sciences. Anyone can admire the city-state, but it is mathematics that allows me to recognize that Taormina in Sicily, with a population of 2,000 could be realistically functioning as such, but Watford with 70,000 could not. No square can be built that allows a pre-electronic communication form of democracy to take place, where all voters can be seen and readily given the chance to speak.

Bramall's problem does not lie in the importance and centrality of mathematics for the curriculum but in the tradition that the subject known as 'English' is the key curriculum element. Bramall wants to deprive mathematics of special status but to allow English to continue to have that status. He does that only because his conception of 'English' is of an inter-disciplinary area rather than the more limited concept, now charac-terized by the phrase 'being literate'. English, as taught, involves delib-erations about ends that include moral, political and social questions. This does not remove the need for mathematical understanding in order to reach better decisions, with a richer evidence base than that achievable without the mathematics education, until the age of 16 and beyond. It may be that it is 'English' that is falsely taken for granted, as undeniably always present, in any end to a 'balloon game' (see above, p. 49). Bramall misses the point that mathematics is needed for much effective deliberation to decide ends. Furthermore, 'English' is not delivered as 'the universal medium' subject to achieve a literate state, but as a much more interdisciplinary activity, combining arts and social sciences.

Bramall's line is much stronger when he argues that knowledge of mathematics could be replaced by someone else acting as adviser. This is true, but how do we decide who is to be educated as trusted adviser, and who as a limited thinker? It looks a bit like 'Brave New World' to me. Bramall takes his line of argument to be stronger than it is, when he concludes that 'If mathematics is no more than a means of objectively describing and communicating, then, like any other technical service, mathematical work could be delegated to others'. The problem lies in mathematics being the science of possibilities. Bramall mistakenly sees the adviser as only able to give one solution, but in most situations there are a range of interpretations, and making decisions from this advice is feasible but not simple. Like White, Bramall fails to recognize the true nature of mathematics. Richard Smith betrays a similar weakness in Chapter Two.

Chapter Two is very attractive, and if 'basic mathematics' were sufficient for anyone to decide whether they want to take 'mathematics studies', then one might go down Richard Smith's line. However, 'basic mathematics' does not describe mathematics at all, and whether we like it or not, the examples like that of the monk that Richard Smith provides are truer descriptions of what mathematics is about than 'learning one's table' is. I did make sure that my children learnt their tables – hopefully as fun – but only to help them have greater confidence when tackling the kinds of problems that Richard Smith describes, and which represent mathematics as it truly is.

As Ormell has written:

> Sheer practicality, though experienced as a potent balm if one is stuck in a practical jam, loses much of its appeal when approached on a merely vicarious basis. Most of the 'questions' done by pupils in classrooms are, inevitably, of the merely vicarious 'practical' variety.
>
> (Ormell, 1999)

The classic image of this difficulty is the description of the child vendors of Brazil in Nunes and Bryant (1996) who have no problem with complicated financial transactions in the street but get '12 + 38' as '130' in the classroom – by the process, *8 + 2 = 10, put down '0' and carry '1'; 8 + 3 + 1 and the '1' that was carried, gives '13'.* No one there had appreciated that 'real problems' can be tackled in the classroom just as if they were occurring outside. Too many pupils, and not just those in Brazil, struggle in the classroom to find the right algorithm, rather than employing their perfectly good alternative strategy. The line of argument found in this chapter is equally relevant to any country's education system and not just to England. The key position of mathematics within the compulsory curriculum is universally justified, as one would hope from a philosophically based argument.

Mathematics, as noted earlier, is special, because it helps one to illuminate the world in a way that no other discipline does. All pupils have to achieve differing levels of competence in mathematical modelling for them to have true fascination with what mathematics uniquely offers. Richard Noss has made the point that through mathematics there can be a greater chance of error-free communication between departments in a company. He noted in passing the need to have effective communication through forms of mathematics between what is taught in schools as mathematics and what is used in the outside world.

The kind of mathematics that is validly required compulsorily throughout a child's education is one that helps in interpreting the world and issues that arise for debate, particularly at Key Stage 4. Where there are such 'real problems' for both teacher and learner then the views expressed in *Better Mathematics* (Ahmed, 1987) are more likely to be fulfilled:

> Teachers need to be seen by pupils to be genuinely interested in their mathematical ideas. We have found that this encourages children to ask and answer their own questions. There is a wealth of strategies for enabling pupils to do more of the thinking in mathematics lessons.
>
> (Ahmed, 1987: 19)

It is crucial to see that the ongoing message from Cockcroft in 1982 remains cogent today, that mathematics is a living subject for both natural science or citizenship debates, and not just a system of learned algorithms. This is still a key message of the National Numeracy Strategy, as well as of the new proposals for the National Curriculum. The strategy has the task of ensuring that 75 per cent of 11 year olds have basic computational skills, but it does not stop there for either the strategy, or the new National Curriculum. As is stated in the advice for parents (*At Home with Numeracy*), 'mathematics is foremost an activity of the mind' (Department for Education and Employment, 1999: 11). The distinctive contribution of mathematics to the school curriculum outlines its importance for reasoning and computation, as well as its importance for modelling situations. As the recent review of the National Curriculum suggests:

> Different cultures have contributed to the development and application of mathematics. Today, the subject transcends cultural boundaries and its importance is universally recognized. Mathematics helps us to understand and change the world.
>
> (Department for Education and Employment/Qualifications and Curriculum Authority, 1999)

This is comparable to what Richard Noss describes in his inaugural lecture, when he is referring to a changed view in industry, from expecting less of an employee because of technology, to expecting more. Incidentally, teachers presently may be experiencing a similar transition, and hopefully soon will be 're-professionalized'. Ahmed states:

> Lack of control has led teachers to question their capabilities. We have found that when teachers have been actively involved in developing and modifying their own assessment procedures – they begin to trust their own judgment, and realize their own expertise.   (Ahmed, 1987: 70)

Noss (1997) makes the point about counter operators:

> Their problem is not that they cannot calculate, not that they cannot 'add up', but they have no *model* of the system. ... The key issue here is that judgment and calculation are often conceived as opposed. ... It will mean that the distinction between domain-specific knowledge of mathematical facts and generalizable skills will become increasingly

obsolete. And for our teaching of numeracies, it will involve constructing new educational cultures in which individuals have the means to
make sense of the models, and the means to express them algebraically,
geometrically, and computationally. (Noss, 1997: 15–17)

Teaching mathematics is not easy. It does involve a depth of understanding and access to a wealth of examples, so that what Richard Smith
describes as 'exceptional circumstances' actually become the norm. It is
the provision of high-quality mathematics education that is challenging,
but surely this is a better state than continuing to find it socially acceptable to say 'I found it hard at school' or 'I am scared of algebra'. Those
same people would never admit to being illiterate, but fearlessly state that
they are not adequately numerate. We have to admit that the weakness
traditionally found in mathematics education reflects a nation in which
mathematics has not been taken sufficiently seriously. We need to be
taught it well until the age of 16 and perhaps longer, so that those who
influence the next generation will be positive about mathematics and that
no one in education will proudly admit their lack of numeracy. This may
well imply that as a nation we should not be satisfied with Level 4 for
75 per cent of the population by the age of 11, but require 75 per cent of
the population at Level 5 or a GCSE Grade D or better in mathematics,
by the age of 16. This may be part of achieving a state in which few
people shy away from picking out the mathematical implications of a
situation, that is, to be happy to read and interpret the text, but to ignore
the data or graphs. Those same people would not announce: 'I can't
read!' or 'I am scared to read some parts!'

Consideration has to be given to what the secondary mathematics curriculum of the year 2020 will be like. This has been emphasized in Butt
(1999), where the author rightly notes the bravery of a Secretary of State
who would allow Key Stage 4 teachers to discuss Turing's identification
of insoluble problems in mathematics. Teachers can do that already. The
key move is to recognize that such discussions ought to be part of the
compulsory curriculum.

Pupils need to work with mathematics, until they reach the point where
they can discuss, with ease, information presented in the text, numerically.

By the end of Key Stage 3, few have reached this point and, hence, the need for mathematics, right to the end of compulsory education, is reinforced. The argument is not one about 'quantities of mathematics' to be taught, but the achieved confidence to use the illuminating power of mathematics in all areas of life, particularly within those pertaining to the natural and social sciences.

9 Another mathematician's apology

Tony Parsons

A personal viewpoint

I stand in awe of professional mathematicians, and yet have the temerity to teach mathematics.

I have an image of myself working in the Wren Library at Trinity College, Cambridge, more than 30 years ago. Isaac Newton's statue is appraising me from the centre of the room, and *A Mathematician's Apology* (Hardy, 1967) is prompting me from the bookshelf behind.

I remember struggling to comprehend a particular mathematical concept. I had a mental block which felt physical: my brain would not cope with it. I recognized a limitation in my brainpower. Maybe with some help at that time I could have progressed further, but it was surely a gate shutting on me. That does not prevent me from enjoying my mathematics, or from being challenged by mathematics in situations I can understand, or from passing on that challenge and enthusiasm to others.

I hold grand masters at chess and bridge in similar respect. I have a block against seeing more than three moves or tricks ahead, yet again I enjoy playing and consider myself capable of teaching others. On the other hand, my abilities at writing, music, languages, art and sport are sufficiently limited that I would feel inhibited, and even incapable, of teaching beyond a very basic level (probably lower than the basic arithmetic which John White (see Chapter Six) says will be largely acquired by the end of primary school). Yet I am happy to call myself a bridge player, a writer, a musician, a linguist, an athlete and an artist within the context of non-professional recreation, and with some training may be able to teach all of those to a reasonable level. There remains, however, a question about the level of competence expected of a teacher, and the consequent enthusiasm: we should be careful whom we entrust to teach mathematics.

We cannot all win Nobel prizes for Literature, nor Olympic Gold Medals, nor Field Medals for Mathematics. We can all aspire to be mathematicians.

The viewpoints of others

The instrumental reasons for learning mathematics are well analysed by John White, although he restricts his analysis to arithmetic. He says only a minority of students will pursue mathematics-based careers, and we have no reason to think that everyone will require mathematical abilities in their jobs. Why, then, is a significantly higher level being asked for at present by both employers and tertiary course directors? A good GCSE grade is more than the basic level which he regards justifies compulsory teaching. Could it be that mathematical ability is universally seen as a measure of useful brain power?

However, what of those who cannot get a C Grade? Some people think it good that only 7 per cent of 16 year olds do not take GCSE mathematics: it may be bad. There may be more suitable courses, which they would find more *fun*. Unfortunately, parental pressure often leads to too many taking GCSE, too many taking the Intermediate tier (aspiring to a C Grade) and too many taking the Higher tier (aspiring to an A). Meanwhile academics complain that the Intermediate tier contains insufficient material for a B Grade, as it bears little resemblance to the old O level.

Poor examination performance becomes the focus of government policy, especially when international comparisons are made. Yet many papers presented at mathematics education conferences (e.g. ICME 8, 1996) by delegates from the Far East demonstrate that an understanding of mathematical process is their goal in preparing children for the future and recognize that cultural differences account for different learning styles, and hence different test results.

Why should one be a mathematician? Why try to acquire such understanding? Can it be acquired at school?

One answer is similar to the rationale for climbing mountains or running marathons, namely you don't know until you've done it. The feelings of achievement are well presented by Richard Smith in Chapter Two, but they are attainable by everyone – there is no exclusivity.

He goes on to argue that what is done in school is of little use, but this applies to Shakespeare and history, too; and when did you last add ammonia to copper sulphate solution? The limited nature of conventional education within the constraints of a compulsory system is well analysed elsewhere (Gardner, 1993). It is like an assembly line, with classes in different subjects controlled by the clock and not the task. Just like the assembly line, it will be overtaken by new technology.

Good teachers, of whatever subject, will keep trying to convey their enthusiasm and insight, despite the pressure to conform to teacher-led 'handle-turning'. All of us are experts on teaching because we have all been taught. Everyone is an expert on teaching mathematics, although many have been taught badly. Poor teachers produce insecurity, whereas good teachers produce enthusiasm. Mathematics enthusiasts may become good teachers if they are not first seized by an industry desperately short of such talent. Meanwhile, misguided parents spend money on commercial rote-learning 'math' packages that drill children in the skills they think are needed, even when the teaching at school is of high quality.

Luckily, mathematics 'failures' are often given second chances on vocational courses that they enjoy but may not recognize as mathematics.

Is mathematics educative, and what is a good teacher?

To answer these questions, I will consider in turn three criteria (due to Peters, 1966):

1 something of value must be passed on;
2 the educatee must care about the subject-matter; and
3 the subject-matter must have a wide cognitive perspective.

The value of mathematics

Like the word 'science', mathematics means knowledge, and by convention knowledge of a certain kind. However, there is a more subtle meaning – mathematics is the *process* and not the end result. It is the *doing* that brings the understanding, seeing the common structure, the common pattern. Ian Stewart, in his 1997 Royal Institution Christmas Lectures, examined the process of mathematizing a problem, and how mathematics relates to the natural world. Why, for example, is the plant world obsessed with Fibonacci numbers, and what is their relationship to the Golden Ratio, which enthralled Renaissance artists, Baroque composers and Ancient Greek architects? His conclusion: 'Magic. ... patterns in our heads that ... capture patterns of the universe around us' (Stewart, 1997: 2).

Historically, it 'is a subject held in high esteem, which has traditionally occupied an unchallenged role within our culture' (see Chapter Six). Students in the Middle Ages studied the seven liberal arts of Roman culture: the 'quadrivium' consisted of arithmetic and geometry, together with astronomy and music. Tony Buzan (1993: 33) lists the following key mental skills: language, number, logic, rhythm, colour, imagery and spatial awareness, three of which are mathematical. He emphasizes that we all have the potential to develop all of them. Howard Gardner proposes:

> At least eight distinct forms of intelligence – defined as the ability to solve problems or fashion products that are valued in at least one cultural setting or community ... linguistic, logical, spatial, musical, bodily kinaesthetic, understanding others, understanding oneself, and apprehension of the natural world. (Gardner, 1997: 35)

He notes that the first two are emphasized in schools, and particularly in examinations. They correspond to the English and mathematics prominent in the QCA review referenced by John White. An earlier study by the HMI (1977) used the following checklist of 'areas of experience: the aesthetic and creative, the ethical, the linguistic, the mathematical, the physical, the scientific, the social and political, and the spiritual.

There is no doubt about the value of mathematical thinking as a unique discipline alongside the others in the various lists, and none of the chapters in this book denies its value, but the question is whether it should receive the privilege (?) of being compulsory. I have much sympathy with the idea of voluntary, discretionary, chosen, courses in mathematics, and regret the effects of the compulsion forced by many careers and tertiary courses. The alternative is, for some, a shallow world without the richness of mathematics, its unique ability to solve their own problems and the opportunity to increase brainpower.

> Mathematics arose from the awakening of the human soul. But it was not born with utilitarian purposes. The first impulse of this science was the desire to solve the mystery of the universe. Its development came, therefore, from the effort to penetrate and understand the infinite. And even now, after centuries of trying to part the heavy veil, it is the search for the infinite that moves us forward. The material progress of man depends on abstract investigations ... .
>
> Given the profound differences between peoples, such universality is surprising: no religion, moral code, form of government, economic plan, philosophical structure, language, or alphabet can boast of anything like it. Counting is one of the few matters about which men do not differ.   (Tahan, 1994: 97 and 152)

Mathematics is recognized as a universal, objective and timeless communications medium. In comparison, English is relative and subjective. A piece of geometry from Ancient Egypt or a piece of algebra in a modern Japanese text are both intelligible throughout the world. This contrasts with national language, its dialects and contemporary vocabulary. The shorthand of 'F = ma' is significantly easier than Newton's statement of his second law in the *Principia*, and its various translations.

There is less justification for non-compulsory mathematics than for non-compulsory English.

Pupils (and teachers) who care
If the pupil is enthusiastic about her mathematics, then the teaching was good. If a child is successful, her confidence builds, she enjoys the subject, she cares about it. Especially among children of lower ability a good teacher will create situations where they can develop their own math-

ematics, where they can solve their own problems, where they can build logical links with what they already understand and see new patterns, where what they do is valued and not 'wrong'. The excitement which Richard Smith describes is not restricted to an elite. Although much experience of school mathematics is 'learning to turn the handle and grind out the results', it does not have to be like that, and good teachers aspire to much more. Smith makes a crucial point about mathematical insight: it is no good the teacher assuring the pupil that it is right; as in English, the meaning of a poem is diminished if it requires explication. The best teachers I have known, who taught me a lot although I was their mentor, have been so interesting, challenging and inspirational, that they held their classes in the palms of their hands.

One of them believes that mathematics is evolutionary, organic, real and living, and that the teacher is responsible for leading the children through all its embryonic stages towards our current understanding.

> First you have the natural numbers. The ones that are whole and positive. The numbers of the small child. But human consciousness expands. The child discovers longing. And do you know what the mathematical expression is for longing? ... The negative numbers. ... the child discovers the in-between spaces ... fractions. ... irrational numbers are infinite. They can't be written down. They force human consciousness out beyond the limits. ... It doesn't stop. It never stops. It's like a vast open landscape. The horizons. You head towards them and they keep receding. (Hoeg, 1996: 101)

Mathematics is about process, it is about solving problems that the pupil accepts as her own. There are three approaches to a solution:

1 the light bulb: flash of inspiration, too rare for most of us, but beautiful when it happens;
2 the T-shirt: we've been there, done that – we've seen it before, so we know the 'trick', usually the result of someone else's inspiration; with insight we can transfer it, and use it in a different context; and
3 the sausage machine: we know a technique which will eventually work if we keep turning the handle.

We need to practise the third so that we have the confidence to let our imagination work and make the first two more likely. The good teacher will highlight situations where the same pattern occurs in differing contexts, because the second approach needs practice too, and depends on linking together ideas that may be stored in different parts of the brain. The good teacher uses investigations a lot, so that any new techniques become part of a pupil's tool-kit for solving her own problem, and not 'somebody else's mathematics' that has to be practised.

In 1994 Andrew Wiles' elegant solution to Fermat's last theorem:

> Brought together virtually all the breakthroughs in twentieth-century number theory.... He created completely new mathematical techniques and combined them with traditional ones in ways that had never been considered possible. ... You turn to a page and there's a brief appearance of some fundamental theorem by Deligne and then you turn to another page and in some incidental way there's a theorem by Hellengouarch.   (Singh, 1997: 304)

This is truly awesome mathematics, as far removed from Richard Smith's examples as they are from many classrooms, yet the excitement and feeling of personal satisfaction is the same, and it uses these same three approaches which are, and should be, available to everyone.

Mathematics everywhere

As Steve Bramall (see Chapter Four) says, it is hard to think of any human experience which is not amenable to mathematical description and analysis. Solving problems is the application of mathematics, and there are many examples (most of these are from Stewart, 1997).

1 What day of the week is New Year 2005?
2 Why is the angle between successive primordia in plants 137.5°?
3 How do you get a wolf, a goat and a cabbage across a river in a small boat?
4 If the TV game show host shows you a door behind which is a goat, should you change your opinion about which door leads to a car?
5 How many different wallpaper patterns are there?

6 How do animals walk, trot, run?
7 This sentence is false????
8 Which method of tying shoelaces uses the least lace?
9 What is the best design for a non-drip teapot, an electronic drum-kit, a classical guitar?
10 How should a fielder run to catch a cricket ball?
11 What does the frequency of road accidents depend on?
12 What is the best strategy for crossing a busy road (at a controlled junction)?

However, *doing* mathematics is like playing a game – within a strict logical framework, *you* decide the playing area and the starting position and *you* decide how you win. The professional mathematicians call the starting position 'axioms', but winning is largely a subjective judgment on how interesting the game is. Everyone likes to keep their brain active, develop its capabilities, and there are many different pastimes, *all* of which have significant mathematical content. No one stops doing mathematics, even (especially!) after formal mathematics teaching finishes ... μανθανω *ergo sum* or, rather, 'I am, therefore I mathematize'!

John White has adopted a logical structure for his chapter: in form at least his thesis is similar to Wiles's, and demonstrates philosophy's debt to mathematics. It seems, however, that he finds Fred Clarke easier to dismiss than Plato and Descartes, while the Pythagorean view is evidently alive and well in Stewart's writing. I cannot resist playing his game, to win by his own rules. In the second section of the chapter he gives three criteria for 'elevating' mathematics above music, art, history and geography in the curriculum, and asks whether mathematics should be compulsory for *one or other* of the three. Logically, he should find a single subject which has a greater claim than mathematics on *all three* criteria, rather than finding a single criterion for each of the other subjects. On his current argument, the justification for elevating mathematics above history might be reason a); above music, reason b); and above art, reason c).

Similarly, Steve Bramall's chapter demonstrates in both its content and form a huge debt to mathematics and mathematical processes. He can't beg to differ about 'mathematical knowledge' without bringing the idea of rational disagreement into disrepute. A pity he does not recognize that there is more mathematics in the latter *process* than in the former structure. Are 'ends' more essential than means? I think many philosophers might disagree – the *process* of living in the present is the more important. Is there no place for fun and games in his austere vision? Isn't he worried that a mathematically based computer model can beat a grandmaster at chess? What is a 'real' square – the Platonic ideal with no thickness or what exists in the 'real' world? Which is the model?

Why learn mathematics?

Buzan says:

> The more (brain connections,) tracks and pathways you can create and use, the clearer, faster and more efficient your thinking will become. The boundaries of human intelligence can, in many ways, be related to the brain's ability to create and use such patterns.   (Buzan, 1993: 29)

He advocates the use of 'mind-maps' to summarize information in a way the brain can easily assimilate, and bringing in as many of his mental skills as possible.

The pattern recognition, the insight developed in mathematical thinking, mirrors this precisely: investigating combinations of coins to pay for parking and recognizing Fibonacci numbers; seeing that a problem in complex number may be viewed from the various viewpoints of Euclidean geometry, vectors, polar co-ordinates, Cartesian co-ordinate geometry and thence algebraic manipulation; and Andrew Wiles's feat, which also showed that the mathematics of modular forms is equivalent to that of elliptic equations, two huge areas of mathematical development, hitherto unconnected but now a key element in 'Grand Unified Mathematics'.

Why learn mathematics?

- Because that's the way the universe is.
- Because that's the way the brain is.
- Because that's the way the mind works.

- Because you can't stop doing mathematics.
- Because everyone wants to develop their brainpower.
- Because everyone likes playing games.

Conclusions

Too many people say they cannot do mathematics because they do not recognize their own mathematical processes. Too many people have not enjoyed success at mathematics, have not known the excitement of solving a problem or spotting a pattern. Too many people try to teach mathematics without confidence, and inculcate a fear of failure. Too many able and enthusiastic mathematicians are put off teaching by the system of education, where assembly-line schooling and examination-training impede the development of the brain. These are not reasons for dropping mathematics from the compulsory curriculum, but for rediscovering the meanings of mathematics and education.

10 Mathematics for all: the way it spozed to be?

John MacBeath

It was in my second year of high school that I first put the question to my teacher 'Why do we have to do mathematics, sir?' He replied that if I ever wanted to go to university I would need to 'have it' as one of my subjects. 'Having mathematics' was certainly one way of thinking about the subject and such a perspective did contribute, unhelpfully, to frame our schoolboy attitudes to learning. Not entirely satisfied with that line of reasoning, however, I offered a second proposition: 'What if I don't want to go to university? Or what if I want to study philosophy or French or zoology?' My teacher, who had apparently never been posed with this question in half a lifetime of teaching moved rapidly to a second line of defence to the effect that he did not have to justify his subject, nor for that matter the ancient wisdom of the school curriculum, to a 14-year-old.

A decade or so later reading James Herndon (1968) I was to discover that this was quite simply 'the way it spozed to be'. Herndon's book about the unquestionable rightness of the status quo casts the issue in a different mould, describing the corollary to the quizzical schoolboy's dilemma. His book is about a progressive young teacher in Harlem who tried in vain to encourage his class to think, to challenge their teacher, to ask their own questions, but was persistently met with the stock response 'That ain't the way it spozed to be, Mr Herndon'.

Much later again I was to be reminded powerfully of the strength of people's attachment to the way things are spozed to be. In 1998 I wrote a somewhat tongue-in-cheek piece for the *Observer*, teasing the sacrosanctity of mathematics' place in the core curriculum and reprising my 14-year-old's question. I suggested that children be encouraged to ask 'Why are you teaching me this today?', citing Postman and Weingartner's (1970) famous appeal for pupils to be armed with built-in crap detectors. The flood of responses to the article ranged from the nostalgic through the congratulatory to the outraged. Among them were 20 letters from pupils in a German school in Paederborn. These sixth formers had been set as their homework task a personal response to the article, addressed to its author. The most touching and revealing from a 17 year old in his final pre-university year of school contained these words:

> It is a very Utopian idea that you have, that people should be encouraged to think for themselves. I do not think it is a good idea because that would be the end of our society as we know it.

It might be argued that there is small cause for celebration of society 'as we know' it or for an educational system which so often betrays itself as hostile to thought. Evidence comes in the starkest form from a source that ought perhaps to 'know' better than a German schoolboy – England's Chief Inspector of Schools. Using the *Observer* piece as a launch pad for his annual invective, Her Majesty's Chief Inspector pronounced my quizzical article high heresy, and the man who perpetrated it, as 'at the heart of the darkness' in British education. It was an awesome reminder of the power of a new orthodoxy, intolerant of thought and unwelcoming of points of view other than its own. It brought to mind the words, attributable as I remember to Peter Medawar, 'a mind so well equipped with the means of refutation that no new idea has the tenacity to seek admittance'.

The article had been spurred by my continuing four-decade-long quest for a well-reasoned answer to my question. Why mathematics for all? Why do we require all young people to continue with mathematics long after it has lost purpose, relevance and interest for them? Have we not learned anything in the last half century? Why do we stick with such tenacity to the inclusion of mathematics in the core curriculum when many other disciplines or areas of study have an equal or more justifiable place? The question has never met, to my satisfaction, with a convincing justification including from informed sources within OFSTED, the QCA, the Standards and Effectiveness Unit of the DfEE. Replies have included the Royal Gambit ('Because it is the Queen of the Sciences'), the MacEnroe Defence ('You can't be serious'), the Cannibal Conjunction ('So that you can become a teacher and teach it to other people'), and the Vocational Prevarication ('It is important for doctors, chemists, architects, accountants, etc.'). The instrumental arguments tend to be the most spurious, while the Platonic arguments, advocating the intrinsic truth and beauty of mathematics are no more than special pleading.

Years, indeed decades after my impertinent, but highly pertinent, question to my mathematics teacher I discovered that I could enjoy mathematical books and puzzles. I read Fermat's Last Theorem and had no difficulty in understanding the obsessional fixation with Fermat's mathematical conundrum. I could sympathize with the discipline of mind that could devote years to the pursuit of a solution, sacrificing personal, social and family life in the search for the combination of numbers that no one before had put into the same sequence. It was intellectually awesome and within its own frame of reference inspiring but, 'out there' in the social world where 99.9 per cent of the population live, it seemed an esoteric and self-indulgent exercise. Could it be seen, in some senses, as a metaphor for school mathematics?

Repacking the curriculum container

Over the years, the curriculum has been unpacked and repacked, more often in the virtual than in the real world. One of the latest examples comes from the Royal Society for the Arts which, in 1999, proposed a quite radical restructuring, suggesting five broad areas of competences: for learning, for citizenship, for relating to people, for managing situations, for managing information. Within this structure there is no place for mathematics as such but a pragmatic case for basic statistical techniques, probability, and concepts of interest and return.

When we engage in this kind of back-to-basic, exercise the first step is to empty the curriculum box and scatter its contents around. The task of repacking then starts with Herbert Spencer's question 'What knowledge is of most worth?' Language and literature, of course, because language, written and spoken, is the very stuff of life and without literature our lives would be threadbare indeed. Mathematics, naturally, because it offers other languages – powerful symbolic languages – and, with the invention of a binary code, has given access to a truly transformational technology. Science, imperatively, because it introduces us both to deep outer space and deep inner space, introducing us to methodology and furnishing tools to explore the very origins of our small selves and of the infinite universe.

History, without doubt, because we are what we are, where we are and where we are going because of our past; and because without understanding of the past our present and future are beyond our reach, and without insight we are destined to relive the errors of our past. Religion, self-evidently, because it is concerned with the very meaning of existence. It is the primary driving force of so many people's lives, the source of inspiration and damnation, the single most contentious area of controversy both historically and in contemporary society, the root of wars, holy and unholy, and the underpinnings of much present day charity and intolerance.

Music, for certain, because it is so significant for the very quality of social life; for its healing and exhilarative powers, because it is the most pervasive aspect of modern living, consuming more hours per day of young people's time, and money, than any other single source. Art too, because, together with music it is the oldest most durable form of cultural expression, liberating, challenging, deeply absorbing and immensely accessible to all. Psychology, because it is about understanding ourselves, our emotions, our thinking and behaving, our relationships with other people in social, organizational and industrial contexts where the concepts of psychology have penetrated every level of human discourse. Politics, because it might help us to consider what levels of poverty are tolerable in advanced capitalism, what 'capitalism' is, what 'socialism' was, what these words mean and why they are so fearfully avoided by a Labour government.

Economics, not only because globalization is taking over our lives, but also because, as Margaret Thatcher taught us, there is an important relationship between the micro and macro business of making and moving money. Foreign languages, each with a different claim, mastery of any one providing an escape route from the rigidity and insularity of one's own linguistic culture. Environmental studies, because our future is intimately bound up with the future of the planet and there is scope for knowledgeable and concerned individuals to make a global difference. Philosophy, because it helps us with our most precious human gift, the ability to think, to reason, to wonder, to ask intelligent questions and understand more deeply the paucity of arguments such as 'because that is the way it spozed to be'.

To say nothing of media studies, drama and dance, health and physical education and much more too. Then there is, of course, something that has come to be called information and communication technology (ICT), which is a very small name for a concept so enormous that without it half the population of the world would collapse like puppets whose strings had been snipped.

We might even want to add in 'education', because we might then be able to give our pupils a meta-perspective on themselves and their schools and on the wonder and absurdity of the entity that is called the curriculum.

In the real world of school policy and politics-making where curriculum is king and queen, two items are generally not emptied from the box before the exercise begins. All the pieces have to be squeezed back into it because English and mathematics are already *in situ*. They are seen as the pillars of school education, symbolically representing the twin deities of current government priorities – literacy and numeracy. Yet the logic of this is not self-evident. While English continues to have a fairly close connection with functional literacy, the link between mathematics and functional numeracy becomes increasingly tenuous as children progress through school. Although both disciplines, it might be claimed, help pupils to move progressively deeper and more critically into the 'real world', that is the world in which understanding and intellectual curiosity mature and in which knowledge becomes action – the case for mathematics is precarious.

The case is a precarious one because the arguments for its inclusion appeal to a Socratic age, a Renaissance era or even mid-twentieth-century context and they are no longer sustainable. And the primary reason for this is the very thing that mathematics helped to create – ICT. It has liberated mathematicians and ordinary people from the tedious calculations that were once obstacles to be hurdled *en route* to the desired destination. Programming is a useful metaphor. In the early days of personal computers access to any higher level functioning was through basic programming. Had the technology not advanced so rapidly, we would have been insisting on basic programming for all. However, a decade or so on we no longer need to know about programming and even programmers themselves are offered so many packaged shortcuts that they rarely need to go back to basics. Statisticians need no longer to calculate standard deviations or squares of chi. They simply need to know what they mean and how to use them.

What all of this demonstrates is that the model of the curricular box has outlived its usefulness. It cannot be expanded and its content cannot be reduced into ever-smaller fragments to accommodate everything that the box should contain. We have to think differently about the nature and purpose of what we teach and what we might have to do very differently in the future. We will have factor into the equation what we know about pupils, their social world and their experience of school life and learning.

Pupils' experience of school mathematics tends to be as a series of problems of increasing difficulty and abstraction to which the right answers have to be found. Numbers come to assume some inherent meaning and mystique for them. They are not hypothetical propositions about which you could have a good argument. They are seen as 'facts' (the ultimate defence in any argument – 'just as two and two equal four') but rarely is the mathematics they acquire seen as helping to explain things in their social world. Mathematics exists within the esoteric world of the mathematics classroom and textbook but not in the experiential world of mathematical principles in which snooker balls ricochet lawfully into pockets, footballs curve gracefully behind defensive walls, goalkeepers (with intuitive application of geometry) narrow the angles, while jazz musicians make music according to mathematical formulae.

For pupils the experience of mathematics is generally bereft of deeper understanding or application, not because of the lack of inspiration among teachers, who in a better world might teach mathematics in the snooker hall, on the hockey field or the building site, but because understanding mathematics is a luxury. It is a luxury which time and logistics cannot afford. There is so much to 'cover', increasingly intricate problems to be solved. So pupils learn at a fairly elementary stage to manipulate $x = 1$ and to 'solve' more and more complex constructions built on this basic premise. However, they are typically lost for words when posed with the question 'What does "equal" mean? Does it mean that x is 1 or that x mirrors 1?' or perhaps 'Let us propose for the sake or argument that x be treated as a 1 until we find out otherwise.'

In the minds of children the world of numbers comes to be seen not as a metaphor, not as a set of hypotheses and constructs, but simply the 'way it spozed to be' and in no conceivable system could two and two ever equal five, even if we wanted them to.

This deterministic view of the world is helped along by the logical, ruthlessly cumulative, world of mathematics. However, the tyranny of the logical/mathematical 'intelligence' is not so much a product of mathematics teaching as the space given to it on the timetable, out of all proportion to its relevance, importance and instrumental value; at the same time, paradoxically, serving to diminish its intrinsic value.

Disaffection through compulsion and overexposure is, of course, an argument that could be applied to virtually any subject. The deeper-lying problem is the secondary school curriculum itself, the subject barriers which it erects and the mind barriers it helps to create. As long as mathematics is mathematics is mathematics, and mathematics is what you 'do' and 'get done' and 'cover' and 'pass' and then put away with a massive sigh of relief, the mind set will continue to stay set, and the debate over curriculum priority will remain an endless and ever more fruitless debate.

So, why not provide the option of mathematical specialization alongside a more generalized treatment of what mathematics means and how it applies, taught within a social reference frame, just as we might teach art and music to those who have no pretensions to be artists and musicians; or health and physical education for those who will never be professional sports people or athletes. Or science for those who will not be scientists.

A similar case has been made for science by Morris Shamos (1994) in his book *The Myth of Scientific Literacy*. Shamos, former president of the New York Academy of Sciences, argues for a more practical approach that encourages an appreciation of science, its purposes and history, its potential and limitations, its impact on our own environment, its effects on our personal health and social lives. His views find an echo with many science teachers who are concerned that what children take away from their school science lessons is deeply misleading and does disservice to good science. Roland Meighan, once a mathematics teacher himself writes:

> When I was learning mathematics at school, then teaching it in school myself, and then watching my son learn it, the same heretical thought kept occurring, that surely there are better things we could be doing than this. (Meighan, 1998: 30)

Bertrand Russell, hardly a slouch in the mathematics department, was highly critical of the school mathematics 'treadmill' and suggested that there were many more useful things to learn.

It is ironic that a question mark should be placed over the place of mathematics and science at a time when governments around the world are increasingly exercised about their relative performance in the international league tables. The Third International Science and Mathematics Study (TIMMS) has caused much breast beating and soul searching in virtually all countries not placed in the top echelon. The basic assumption is that the mean performance (in more than the statistical sense perhaps) of children at a certain age is an indicator of a country's educational health and, even more tenuously, that it is related to a country's economic performance. Peter Robinson (1998) of the Institute for Public Policy Research has demonstrated the fallacy of this second premise.

Drawing on statistics compiled for the World Bank, he finds no correlation whatever between economic growth and school performance in mathematics. He concludes:

> What could be a sober and informed debate about English education is in danger of being drowned out by the simplistic and often shrill rhetoric which seems to dominate policy making in education.
>
> (Robinson, 1998: 60)

If we wish to find a plausible link between the economy and the state of the art in mathematics and science it is obviously to higher education that we should be turning our attention. There we would find that the United States, George Bush's 'Nation at Risk', on account of its mediocre school performance in mathematics/science, is at the leading edge in both these fields at a university and research level.

The challenge for the schools of the year 2000 is to provide secondary age pupils with an array of rich learning resources from which they can derive meaning and benefit, closing as few doors as possible, keeping open the possibility of mathematical adventuring in life after school. Heretical though it might be, we might consider secondary school mathematics as a potentially attractive extra-curricular activity. Just as music has accepted its place in the voluntary twilight zone of lunchtimes, after school, or on Saturday mornings, why not mathematics? Some schools have managed to produce, out of this optional and extra-curricular time, outstanding orchestras, bands, choirs and solo musicians. A school which could boast an equal number of accomplished mathematicians would be an exceptional school.

In fact, the proposition is not so far-fetched or heretical after all. Such voluntary provision does already exist in many schools in the form of mathematics clubs, study support, supplementary classes and residential weekends or summer schools.

'Who ever would have believed I could do mathematics five hours a day during my summer holidays and still come back for more?' said one secondary age pupil who had attended a summer school at Birmingham's University of the First Age. It was engaging and profitable for her, a self-confessed mathematics phobic, because it was built around practical activities in a context where there was time and space to play at mathematics, free from the relentless demands to 'have it' and to give it back.

Perhaps rather than trying to impose the subject in discrete timetabled blocks we should be seeking new imaginative new ways, Third Millennium ways, of keeping mathematics alive by keeping it firmly in its place.

Bibliography

Ahmed, A. (1987), *Better Mathematics – A Curriculum Development Study*. London: HMSO.

Anderson, E. (1998), 'John Stuart Mill: democracy as sentimental education'. In A.O. Rorty (ed.) *Philosophers on Education: New historical perspectives*. London: Routledge.

Anderson, J. (1999), 'Being mathematically educated in the 21st century: what should it mean?' In C. Hoyles, C. Morgan and G. Woodhouse (eds) *Rethinking the Mathematics Curriculum*. London: Falmer Press.

Andrews, P. (1998), 'Peddling the myth'. *Mathematics in School*, March issue, 27, 2.

Aristotle (1976), *Ethics*. Tr. H. Tredennick. Harmondsworth: Penguin Classic.

Arnot, M., Gray, J., James, M., Rudduck, J. with Duveen, G. (1998) *OFSTED Reviews of Research Recent research on gender and educational performance*. London: HMSO.

Askew, M. (1977), 'Mental methods of computation'. *Mathematics Teaching*, 160.

Ball, S. (1990), *Policy and Policy-Making in Education: Explorations in policy sociology*. London: Routledge.

Barrow, J.D. and Landshoff, P. (1999), 'Helping to bring mathematics alive'. *Cambridge*, 44, 84–87.

Bayliss, V. (1999), *Opening Minds: Education for the 21st century*. London: Royal Society for the Arts.

Bernstein, R.J. (1981/82), 'From Hermeneutics to Praxis'. *Review of Metaphysics*, 35.

Board of Education (1929), *Handbook of Suggestions for the Consideration of Teachers and Others Concerned in the Work of Public Elementary Schools*. London: HMSO.

Bramall, S. (1998), 'Hermeneutic Understanding and the Liberal Aims of Education'. Unpublished Ph.D. Thesis, University of London.

Brown, M. (1996) 'The context of the research – the evolution of the National Curriculum for mathematics'. In D.C. Johnson and A. Millett (eds) *Implementing the Mathematics National Curriculum: policy, politics and practice.* London: Paul Chapman.

Burton, L. (ed.) (1990; rpt. 1992), *Gender and Mathematics: An international perspective.* London: Cassell Educational Ltd.

Butt, P. (1999), 'So much better in the Old Days'. *Micromath*, 15/2, The Association of Teachers of Mathematics.

Buzan, T. (1993), *The Mind-Map Book.* London: BBC Books.

Cheng, Y., Payne, J. and Witherspoon, S. (1995), *Science and Mathematics in Full-time Education After 16.* Youth Cohort Report No. 36. London: Department for Education and Employment.

Clarke, F. (1923), *Essays in the Politics of Education.* Oxford: Oxford University Press.

Cockroft (1982), *Mathematics Counts.* Report of the Committee of Inquiry into the Teaching of Mathematics in Schools. London: HMSO.

Cooper, B. (1984), 'On explaining change in school subjects'. In I.F. Goodson and S.J. Ball (eds), *Defining the Curriculum: Histories and ethnographies.* London: Falmer Press.

Cooper, B. (1985), 'Secondary school mathematics since 1950: reconstructing differentiation'. In I.F. Goodson (ed.), *Social Histories of the Secondary Curriculum: Subjects for Study.* London: Falmer Press.

Dales, H.G. and Oliveri, G. (eds) (1998), *Truth in Mathematics.* Oxford: Clarendon Press.

Davis, B. (1995), 'Why teach mathematics? Mathematical education and enactivist theory'. *For the Learning of Mathematics*, 15, 2.

Davis, P.J. and Hersh, R. (1980), *The Mathematical Experience.* Boston: Birkhauser.

Department for Education and Employment (1997), *Excellence in Schools.* London: The Stationery Office.

Department for Education and Employment (1998), *The Implementation of the National Numeracy Strategy: The final report of the Numeracy Task Force.* London: The Stationery Office.

Department for Education and Employment /Qualifications and Curriculum Authority (1999), *The Review of the National Curriculum in England. The Consultation Materials.* London: HMSO.

Descartes, R. (1969 edn), *The Essential Descartes.* Wilson, M.D. (ed.). New York: New American Library.

Devlin, K.J. (1998), *Mathematics: The new golden age.* London: Penguin.

Dubbey, J.M. (1970), *Development of Modern Mathematics.* London: Butterworths.

Edge, A. and West, A. (1998), 'Testing Britain against Europe'. *Parliamentary Brief*, 5, 5.

Effros, E. (1998), 'Mathematics as language'. In H.G. Dales and G. Oliveri (eds), *Truth in Mathematics*. Oxford: Clarendon Press.

Elliott, R.K. (1975), 'Education and human being'. In S.C. Brown (ed.), *Philosophers Discuss Education*. London: Macmillan.

Ernest, P. (1986), 'Social and Political Values'. *Mathematics Teaching*, 116.

— (1991), *The Philosophy of Mathematics Education*. London: Falmer Press.

— (1998), *Social Constructivism as a Philosophy of Mathematics*. Albany: New York: SUNY Press.

Evens, H. and McCormick, R. (1998), 'The use of mathematics in secondary school D&T'. Unpublished paper, British Educational Research Association annual conference, available at http://www.leeds.ac.uk/educol/documents/000000808.htm.

Fennema, E. (1990), 'Justice, equity and mathematics education'. In D. Fennema and G.C. Leder (eds), *Mathematics and Gender*. New York and London: Teachers College, Columbia University.

Fehr, H.F. (1996), 'SSMCIS'. *American Mathematics Monthly*, 73, 533.

Fitch, J. (1902), *Lectures on Teaching*. Cambridge: Cambridge University Press.

Foucault, M. (1976), *Discipline and Punish*. Harmondsworth, Penguin.

Gadamer, H.G. (1989), *Truth and Method*. London: Sheed and Ward.

Gallagher, A.M. (1997), *Educational Achievement and Gender: A review of research evidence on the apparent underachievement of boys*. Bangor, Co Down: Department of Education, Northern Ireland.

Gardner, H. (1993), *The Unschooled Mind*. London: Fontana.

— (1997), *Extraordinary Minds*. London: Weidenfeld & Nicolson.

Gordon, P. and Lawton, D. (1978), *Curriculum Change in the Nineteenth and Twentieth Centuries*. London: Hodder and Stoughton.

Goulding, M. (1995), 'GCSE coursework in mathematics: teachers' perspectives and the performance or girls'. *Evaluation and Research in Education*, 9, 3.

Graham, D. (1996), *The Education Racket: Who cares about the children?* Glasgow: Neil Wilson.

Graham, D., Graham, C. and Whitcombe, A. (1984; revised 1995, rpt. 1998), *A Level Mathematics*. London: Letts Educational.

Hamlyn, D.W. (1967), 'The logical and psychological aspects of learning'. In R.S. Peters (ed.), *The Concept of Education*. London: Routledge & Kegan Paul.

Hammersley, J.M. (1968), 'On the enfeeblement of mathematical skills by "modern mathematics" and by similar soft intellectual trash in schools and universities'. *Bulletin of the Institute of Mathematics and its Applications*, 4.

Hans, N. (1951), *New Trends in Education in the Eighteenth Century*. London: Routledge and Kegan Paul.

Hardy, G.H. (1967), *A Mathematician's Apology*. Cambridge: Cambridge University Press.

Harris, M. (December 1997), 'Mathematics for all?'. *Mathematics Teaching*, 161.

Hirst, P. (1965), 'Liberal education and the nature of knowledge'. In R.D. Archambault (ed.), *Philosophical Analysis and Education*. London: Routledge and Kegan Paul.

HMI (1977), *Curriculum 11–16*. London: HMSO.

— (1979), *Mathematics 5 to 11: A handbook of suggestions*. London: DES.

Herndon, J. (1968), *The Way it Spozed to Be*. New York: Wiley.

Hoeg, Peter (1996), *Miss Smilla's Feeling for Snow*. London: Harvill.

Howson, G. (1982), *A History of Mathematics Education in England*. Cambridge: Cambridge University Press.

Howson, G., Keitel, C. and Kilpatrick, J. (1981), *Curriculum Development in Mathematics*. Cambridge: Cambridge University Press.

Hoyles, C., Morgan, C. and Woodhouse, G. (eds) (1999), *Rethinking the Mathematics Curriculum*. London: Falmer Press.

Høyrup, J. (1987), 'Influences of institutionalized mathematics teaching on the development and organization of mathematical thought in the pre-modern period'. In J. Fauvel and J. Gray (eds), *The History of Mathematics: A reader*. London: Macmillan.

Huckstep, P. (1999), 'How can mathematics be useful?'. *Mathematics in School*, 28.

ICME (1996), *Short Presentations*, 8. Seville.

James, W. (1981 edn), *The Principles of Psychology*. Vol 1. Cambridge, Massachusetts: Harvard University Press.

Jeffery, J. (1988), 'Technology across the curriculum: a discussion paper'. Unpublished paper, Exeter: University of Exeter School of Education.

Kline, M. (1972), *Mathematics in Western Culture*. Harmondsworth: Penguin.

Leung, F. (1999), 'The traditional Chinese views of mathematics and education: implications for mathematics education in the new millennium'. In C. Hoyles, C. Morgan and G. Woodhouse (eds), *Rethinking the Mathematics Curriculum*. London: Falmer Press.

Lightbody, P. and Durndell, A. (1996), 'Gendered career choice: is sex stereotyping the cause or the consequence?' *Educational Studies*, 22, 2.

Maclure, J.S. (ed.) (1969), *Educational Documents: England and Wales, 1816–1968*. London: Methuen Educational.

Marcuse, H. (1964), *One Dimensional Man*. London: Routledge and Kegan Paul.

Marks, J. (1996), *Standards for Arithmetic: How to correct the decline*. London: Centre for Policy Studies.

Meighan, R. (1998), 'Educational superstitions of our time'. *Natural Parent*, May.

Monk, R. (1997), *Bertrand Russell*. London: Vintage Books.

Murphy, P.F. and Gipps, C.V. (1996), *Equity in the Classroom. Towards effective pedagogy for girls and boys*. London: Falmer Press/UNESCO Publishing.

National Commission on Education (1993), *Learning to Succeed: A radical look at education today and a strategy for the future. Report of the Paul Hamlyn Foundation*. London: Heinemann.

Niss, M. (1983), 'Mathematics education for the "automatical society"'. In R. Schaper (ed.), *Hochschuldidaktik der Mathematik* (Proceedings of a conference held at Kassel 4–6 October 1983). Alsbach-Bergstrasse, Germany: Leuchtturm-Verlag.

— (1994), 'Mathematics in society'. In R. Biehler, R.W. Scholz, R. Straesser, and B. Winkelmann (eds), *The Didactics of Mathematics as a Scientific Discipline*. Dordrecht: Kluwer

— (1996), 'Goals of Mathematics Teaching'. In A.J. Bishop (ed.), *The International Handbook of Mathematics Education*. Dordrecht: Kluwer Academic, Volume 1.

Noss, R. (1997), *New Cultures, New Numeracies*. London: Institute of Education.

Nunes, T. and Bryant, P. (1996), *Children Doing Mathematics*. Oxford: Blackwell.

OFSTED and the Equal Opportunities Commission (1996), *The Gender Divide: Performance differences between boys and girls at school*. London: HMSO.

Ormell, C.P. (1996), *MAG (Mathematics Applicable Group) News*, 31, December.

— (1999), *MAG (Mathematics Applicable Group) News*, 37, January.

Passmore, J. (1980), *The Philosophy of Teaching*. London: Duckworth.

Pepper, S.C. (1948), *World Hypotheses: A study in evidence*. Berkeley, California: University of California Press.

Peters, R.S. (1966), *Ethics and Education*. London: Allen and Unwin.

Phillips, M. (1996), *All Must Have Prizes*. London: Little, Brown and Company.

Plato (1974), *The Republic*. Tr. D. Lee. Harmondsworth: Penguin.

Postman, N. and Weingartner, C. (1970), *Teaching as a Subversive Activity*. Harmondsworth: Penguin.

Putnam, H. (1982), 'Why Reason can't be naturalized'. *Synthèse*, 52.

Qualifications and Curriculum Authority (1998), *Values, Aims and Priorities of the School Curriculum*. London: QCA.

Robinson, P. (1998), 'Tyranny of the league tables'. *Parliamentary Brief*, 5, 5.

Robitaille, D.F. and Garden, R.A. (eds) (1989), *The IEA Study of Mathematics II: Contexts and outcomes of school mathematics*. Oxford: Pergamon.

Rotman, B. (1993), *Ad Infinitum The Ghost in Turing's Machine: Taking God out of mathematics and putting the body back in*. Stanford, California: Stanford University Press.

Sells, L. (1973), *High School Mathematics as the Critical Filter in the Job Market.* Proceedings of the Conference on Minority Graduate Education, Berkeley: University of California.

Shamos, M. (1994), *The Myth of Scientific Literacy.* New Brunswick: Rutgers University Press.

Siegel, H. (1995), '"Radical" pedagogy requires "conservative" epistemology'. *Journal of Philosophy of Education*, 29, 1.

Singh, S. (1997), *Fermat's Last Theorem.* London: Fourth Estate.

Skovsmose, O. (1994), *Towards a Philosophy of Critical Mathematics Education.* Dordrecht: Kluwer Academic.

Spender, D. (1986), 'Some thoughts on the power of mathematics'. In L. Burton (ed.), *Girls Into Maths Can Go.* London: Holt, Rinehart and Winston.

Stewart, I. (1997), *The Magical Maze.* London: Weldenfeld & Nicolson.

Tahan, M. (1994), *The Man who Counted.* Edinburgh: Cannongate.

Tate, T. (1854), *The Philosophy of Education.* Longman, Brown, Green and Longmans.

Taylor, F.W. (1911), *The Principles of Scientific Management.* London and New York.

Times Educational Supplement (1996), 'Male brain rattled by curriculum "oestrogen"', 15 March.

Toulmin, S. (1958), *The Uses of Argument.* Cambridge: Cambridge University Press

Watson, F. (1909), *The Beginnings of the Teaching of Modern Subjects in England.* London: Pitman.

Walkerdine, V. (1998), *Counting Girls Out: Girls and mathematics* (new edition). London: Falmer Press.

Weber, M. (1986), *Economy and Society.* Berkeley: University of California Press.

Weiner, G. (1985), *Just a Bunch of Girls.* Buckingham: Open University Press.

Wells, D. (1989), 'Why do mathematics?' *Mathematics Teaching*, 127.

Whitcombe, A. (1988), 'Mathematics: creativity, imagination, beauty'. *Mathematics in School*, 17, 2.

Williams, R. (1961), *The Long Revolution.* London: Penguin Books.

Wittgenstein, L. (1977), *On Certainty.* Ed. G.E.M. Anscombe and G.H. von Wright. Oxford: Blackwell.

Written Arithmetic 2, County Examination, Peterborough (27 March 1935), for scholarship entry from junior to secondary school, Peterborough Education Committee. Kindly supplied by Mrs Evelyn E. Cowie, who sat and passed the examination.

Yeldham, F.A. (1936), *The Teaching of Arithmetic through Four Hundred Years (1535–1935).* London: Harrap.

Young, R.M. (1979), 'Why are figures so significant? The role and the critique of quantification'. In J. Irvine, I. Miles and J. Evans (eds), *Demystifying Social Statistics*. London: Pluto Press.